MAKING
CORPORATE REPORTS
VALUABLE

MAKING CORPORATE REPORTS VALUABLE

A Discussion Document by the Research Committee
of The Institute of Chartered Accountants of Scotland
and edited by Peter N McMonnies

The Institute of Chartered Accountants of Scotland

KOGAN PAGE

First published in Great Britain in 1988
by Kogan Page Limited, 120 Pentonville Road, London N1 9JN
by arrangement with The Institute of Chartered Accountants of Scotland,
27 Queen Street, Edinburgh EH2 1LA

Copyright © The Institute of Chartered Accountants of Scotland 1988

British Library Cataloguing in Publication Data
Making corporate reports valuable.
  1. Business report writing
  I. McMonnies, Peter N. II. Institute of
  Chartered Accountants of Scotland
  658.1'512   HF5719

ISBN 1-85091-489-3

This book is published for the Research Committee of The Institute of Chartered Accountants of Scotland and does not necessarily represent the views of the Council of the Institute.

No responsibility for loss occasioned to any person acting or refraining from action as a result of any material in this publication can be accepted by the author or publisher.

All rights reserved. No part of this publication may be reproduced, stored in a retrieval system or transmitted, in any form, or by any means, electronic, mechanical, photocopying, recording or otherwise, without the prior permission of the publishers.

Printed and bound in Great Britain by
Mackays Ltd, Chatham, Kent

Contents

	Paragraphs	Pages
Foreword		10
About the Authors and the Editor		12
Acknowledgements		13
INTRODUCTION	0.1 – 0.14	15
Chapter 1 – BACKGROUND TO OUR SUGGESTIONS	1.1 – 1.17	18
Summary	1.18 – 1.20	21
Chapter 2 – CORPORATE GOVERNANCE AND ITS EFFECTS ON INTERNAL AND EXTERNAL REPORTING	2.1 – 2.11	23
Summary	2.12	25
Chapter 3 – THE PHILOSOPHY, OBJECTIVES AND SCOPE OF INTERNAL AND EXTERNAL CORPORATE REPORTING		26
A Internal reporting	3.1 – 3.4	26
B External users of corporate reports	3.5 – 3.10	27
C Internal and external information needs	3.11 – 3.14	29
D External reporting	3.15 – 3.20	30
E Independent assessment	3.21 – 3.23	31
Summary	3.24 – 3.28	33
Chapter 4 – PROBLEMS OF PRESENT-DAY ACCOUNTS		34
A Conceptual basis	4.1 – 4.2	34
B Objectives of the entity	4.3	34

5

C	Present financial position and performance		35
	(a) Financial position	4.4	35
	(b) Performance		35
	(i) Recognition of income	4.5 – 4.7	35
	(ii) Components of income	4.8 – 4.9	36
	(iii) Segmental reporting	4.10	36
	(iv) Other disclosures	4.11	37
	(c) Market capitalisation	4.12	37
	(d) What is the entity?	4.13	37
	(e) Consolidated financial statements		37
	(i) Business combinations	4.14 – 4.16	37
	(ii) Goodwill	4.17	38
	(iii) The entities in the group	4.18 – 4.19	38
	(f) Comprehensibility	4.20	39
D	Future financial position and performance	4.21 – 4.22	39
E	Economic environment	4.23	40
F	Ownership, management and staff	4.24 – 4.25	40
G	Audit	4.26 – 4.29	41
	Summary	4.30 – 4.32	41

Chapter 5 – SOME POSSIBLE SOLUTIONS   43

	Introduction	5.1 – 5.2	43
A	Conceptual basis	5.3	43
B	Objectives of the entity	5.4 – 5.5	43
C	Present financial position and performance		44
	(a) Financial position	5.6 – 5.8	44
	(b) Performance		44
	(i) Recognition of income	5.9 – 5.11	44
	(ii) Components of income	5.12	45
	(iii) Segmental reporting	5.13 – 5.15	45

		(iv) Related party transactions	5.16	46
		(v) Other disclosures	5.17 – 5.19	46
	(c)	Market capitalisation	5.20 – 5.21	47
	(d)	Consolidated financial statements	5.22 – 5.25	47
	(e)	Associated companies	5.26 – 5.27	48
	(f)	Off-balance sheet financing and window dressing	5.28 – 5.30	49
	(g)	Comprehensibility	5.31 – 5.36	49
D	Future financial position and performance		5.37 – 5.40	51
E	Economic environment		5.41 – 5.44	51
	(a)	The market place	5.42 – 5.43	51
	(b)	Comparative operational statistics	5.44	52
F	Ownership and management		5.45 – 5.46	52
G	Staff resources		5.47 – 5.50	53
H	Audit (independent assessment)			54
	(a)	The report	5.51 – 5.53	54
	(b)	Audit committees	5.54 – 5.56	55
Summary			5.57 – 5.61	55

Chapter 6 – VALUATION OF ASSETS AND LIABILITIES ... 57

Introduction		6.1	57
A	Asset valuation methods available	6.2 – 6.12	57
B	Market capitalisation	6.13 – 6.19	59
C	Use of net realisable values	6.20 – 6.23	61
D	Reasons for disregarding replacement cost	6.24 – 6.26	64
E	Practical considerations in using net realisable values	6.27 – 6.35	65
Summary		6.36 – 6.38	66

Chapter 7 – MEETING THE INFORMATION NEEDS OF MANAGEMENT AND INVESTORS ... 68

Introduction		7.1 – 7.6	68
A	Strategy and planning	7.7 – 7.10	69

	B	Present financial status	7.11 – 7.44	70
		(a) Assets and liabilities statement	7.12 – 7.20	70
		(b) Operations statement	7.21 – 7.22	73
		(c) Statement of changes in financial wealth	7.23 – 7.26	73
		(d) Distributions statement	7.27 – 7.32	74
		(e) Examples	7.33 – 7.34	76
		(f) Cash flow statement	7.35 – 7.38	76
		(g) Necessary segments	7.39 – 7.42	77
		(h) Other necessary information	7.43 – 7.44	78
	C	Future financial status	7.45 – 7.53	79
		(a) Financial plans	7.46 – 7.51	
		(b) Future cash flows	7.52	80
		Summary	7.53	80
	D	Presentation of information		81
		(a) Layering	7.54	81
		(b) Timeliness	7.55 – 7.58	81
	E	Independent assessment	7.59 – 7.68	83
		Summary	7.69 – 7.73	85
Annex 1 –	Examples of the way in which the four basic statements bring out relevant information			85
Annex 2 –	Suggested outline of the contents of an independent assessor's long-form report			89
Chapter 8 –	CONCLUSIONS			92
	A	The case for change	8.1 – 8.4	92
	B	The benefits	8.5 – 8.16	92
		(a) Managements	8.6 – 8.9	93
		(b) External users	8.10 – 8.12	93
		(c) The country as a whole	8.13 – 8.15	93
		(d) Company accountants	8.16	94
	C	The implications	8.17 – 8.31	94
		(a) Managements	8.18 – 8.20	94
		(b) External users	8.21 – 8.22	95
		(c) Governments	8.23 – 8.24	95
		(d) Securities authorities	8.25	95
		(e) Professional accountancy bodies	8.26 – 8.28	96
		(f) Auditors	8.29 – 8.30	96

(g) Researchers	8.31	96
Summary	8.32	97

Chapter 9 – SUMMARY OF OUR
       SUGGESTIONS   98
       Basic conclusions   9.1 – 9.4   98
       Users of corporate reports   9.5 – 9.10   98
       Information for managements   9.11 – 9.16   99
       External reporting   9.17 – 9.46   100
       Long-term improvements in
          reporting internally and
          externally   9.47 – 9.55   102
       Valuation of assets and liabilities 9.56 – 9.59 103
       Independent assessment   9.60 – 9.63   104
       Research needed   9.64 – 9.65   105

Appendix: Vocabulary and Abbreviations   107

Foreword

This publication is the result of a major research project undertaken by the Research Committee of The Institute of Chartered Accountants of Scotland. The Committee is extremely grateful to the Scottish Chartered Accountants' Trust for Education for funding the project.

The project came about following discussions among the members of the Committee about their concern over the lack of a framework for accounting research. As we explored this issue we became aware of inconsistencies in practices in financial reporting and were led to the conclusion that present-day corporate reports are unsatisfactory in that they do not provide information in the right format for readers to use in making judgments.

To help us arrive at our suggestions for improving the information flow to management and between management and investors we went back to basics and undertook certain studies and discussions. We identified, and sought to overcome, what we believe to be the major failings of present corporate reports. We also commissioned literature surveys and a research project. The relevant papers are available in a separate publication.

We believe that, as a result of our deliberations, we have produced a consistent framework for accounting research and have mentioned areas in which we think research would be especially beneficial. We divide our suggestions between those which we think could be adopted, if found acceptable, within the short to medium term and our more tentative long-term suggestions.

We are also sharply aware of the difficulty of reconciling the demands on management to disclose information with their duty

Foreword

to safeguard investors' interests and recognise that sometimes it may be in investors' interests not to disclose. We also acknowledge that although traditional financial data is an important component of control, modern management theory suggests that it is of less importance as a basis of policy formulation.

We hope the whole document will stimulate discussion and experimentation. Such hopes have often been expressed in vain by those who have sought to stimulate change in accounting practice. Roughly parallel instances to the present attempt were *The Corporate Report* (1975) and *Accounting for Stewardship in a Period of Inflation* (1968).

We are grateful to the Project Editor, Peter McMonnies, for his tremendous achievement in pulling together the various threads which emerged from the Committee's numerous debates on the subject. The discussion document has deliberately been written in such a way as to be understandable to readers who are not familiar with the extensive academic theoretical literature.

Jack Shaw
Convener, Research Committee
The Institute of Chartered
Accountants of Scotland

About the Authors and the Editor

This discussion document was prepared by the Research Committee of The Institute of Chartered Accountants of Scotland, which consisted of:

John C Shaw (Convener)
E John Baden
John Baillie
Paul V Boyle
R Gavin Burnett
Andrew M McCosh
Ian C McCutcheon
Norman L Murray
Hamilton Perry
Margaret E Smart
David P Tweedie

Peter N McMonnies acted as Editor. Now retired from practice, he was latterly UK Director of Accounting and Auditing Research with Thomson McLintock & Co. He founded that firm's technical department in 1975, having previously been in charge of accounting and auditing research at The Institute of Chartered Accountants of Scotland. He is a well-known writer on accounting topics.

Members of the Institute's secretariat also involved in the preparation of the document were Aileen E Beattie, Ian F Y Marrian and Isobel N Sharp.

Acknowledgements

The Research Committee would like to express its thanks to a large number of people for their help in preparing "Making Corporate Reports Valuable". In particular, we would thank –

- ★ The Trustees of the Scottish Chartered Accountants' Trust for Education — for providing the necessary financial support

- ★ Ian Fraser
- ★ Paul Gordon
- ★ George Harte
- ★ David Hatherly
- ★ Tom Lee
- ★ Mike Walker
- ★ Pauline Weetman

 — for undertaking literature surveys on specified topics to assist the Committee

- ★ Chris Fletcher
- ★ John Grinyer
- ★ Tom Lee
- ★ David Solomons

 — for commenting on various drafts of the discussion document

- ★ Mark Tippett — who carried out a research project on financial managers' views on changing corporate reporting practices

- ★ Eric Frankis
- ★ Roger Moore
- ★ Robbie Robertson
- ★ Dan White

 — all investment analysts who met with members of the Committee to discuss some aspects of the document's proposals

- ★ Participants at the — who took part in open debate

- Institute's 1987 Summer School
* Sir Robin Duthie
* Sid Gray
* Nigel Macdonald
* Tom Neville
* Ken Peasnell
* John Stevenson
* Geoff Whittington
* The Office-Bearers and Members of Council of the Institute

— on a summary of the draft document

— who "tested to destruction" an early draft of the document

— who commented at the various stages in the preparation of the document

We know that not one of them would agree with every aspect of the final document. Their primary role was to challenge the Committee's thinking. This they did and we are grateful to them all.

Finally, our thanks and commiserations must go to Fiona Wright in the Institute's Accounting and Auditing Department, who has had to type and retype the drafts of this discussion document.

Introduction

0.1 Our objective in producing this discussion document is to improve, in the long term, the quality of measuring and reporting corporate activity. It has been prepared in a spirit of stimulating debate, and ultimately action, on corporate reporting, because our studies, and the discussions which we have had, indicate to us that the present model for corporate reporting is not satisfactory. Our reasons for believing this to be the case are set out briefly in Chapter 1 and in more detail in Chapter 4.

0.2 We stress that this is a document to promote discussion and experimentation. It is in no sense an exposure draft of proposed mandatory requirements. Where we do suggest that some legal (or quasi-legal) rules may be needed, those suggestions, like everything else in the document, are there to be debated.

0.3 We address this document to everyone interested in corporate reporting but principally to those who have to report, those who have to audit and those who have to use corporate reports.

0.4 It is, perhaps, too blindingly obvious to point out that if corporate reports are not useful to someone there is no point in preparing them. What is not so clear is what they should be useful for. We start from the premise that they must provide understandable information – on the stewardship of those charged with the duties of managing business entities and on the performance and standing of those entities – that will enable readers to form valid judgments. We look on them as a help in providing protection for investors and creditors and in making the stock market work efficiently.

0.5 For the purposes of our deliberations we have assumed that we could start with a "clean sheet", that is, we could ignore the existing laws, accounting rules (such as those contained in Statements of Standard Accounting Practice (SSAPs)) and other constraints in order to try to attain what we believe to be the best result. (Obviously such existing constraints cannot be ignored in practice, and we have noted in Chapter 8 some implications of what we shall be suggesting.)

0.6 In this document we have confined our interests to business enterprises which are required by law to report to those who supply their finances – both share and loan capital. In the United Kingdom these are principally companies incorporated under the Companies Acts. (Throughout we shall refer to these enterprises as "entities" unless we are dealing with a specific type, eg private company, nationalised industry.) Non-business entities, whose objectives are different, should, we thought, be providing rather different information and we do not deal with them here.

0.7 We have considered the whole subject principally in a United Kingdom context, but the basic suggestions which we make could have worldwide application. While appreciating that differing laws, customs, economic structures and ideologies have led in the past to different approaches to corporate reporting in some other countries, we believe that the principles on which we have worked are valid and would lead to an improvement in internal and external reporting everywhere.

0.8 Because of the assumption noted in paragraph 0.5 we have tried as far as possible to avoid words which are likely to carry an existing (but possibly misleading) connotation. The reader will not find terms such as "balance sheet", "profit and loss account", "auditor" and the like except where we are referring to something which exists at the moment and is given that specific name.

0.9 We have set out the results of our study in the following way. Chapter 1 explains what motivated us to make the suggestions which we do make for reporting to external users. Then in Chapters 2 and 3 we set the scene by discussing corporate governance, identifying the outside users to whom businesses should report and evaluating their needs and the needs of corporate management for information. We follow this up with a critique of the principal shortcomings in external financial reporting under existing circumstances in Chapter 4. (We appreciate that some of these shortcomings may be temporary, but others are certainly more fundamental.) Then in Chapter 5 we set out possible solutions to problems thrown up by the previous chapter, most of which we think could be adopted, if found acceptable, within a reasonably short space of time.

0.10 From this point onwards our suggestions are more tentative and will need a longer time-span to adopt. They form, however, the most important part of our thinking. They will probably require a greater degree of debate and experimentation, and we hope they

Introduction

will stimulate researchers to follow them up, testing them and their implications in whole or piecemeal. Our discussion on the values which could be applied to assets and liabilities is in Chapter 6 and our suggestions for an entirely new reporting package are set out in Chapter 7.

0.11 The premises on which we have worked in Chapters 6 and 7 are that tinkering with published statements prepared under the historical cost convention is unlikely to help improve the portrayal of economic reality (by which we mean what really happens expressed in financial terms) and that management's information packages do provide information which is useful and can provide guidance for action. We believe that the portrayal of economic reality involves reporting upon an entity's total wealth and upon changes in that wealth during the past and expected in the future.

0.12 Chapter 8, headed "Conclusions", summarises the case for change from the existing regime, the potential benefits from the changes that we suggest and the implications for those concerned; while the final chapter summarises the main suggestions made in previous chapters.

0.13 To help us arrive at our suggestions we commissioned literature surveys and one small research project. The relevant papers are published separately as Volume 2. We also undertook certain studies and discussions ourselves, and we worked through an example of how the suggestions contained in Chapter 7 would turn out in practice. We used comparatively small numbers, which we have inserted in the illustrations in that chapter, but by so doing we were able to satisfy ourselves that our ideas made sense.

0.14 Finally, although we approached the subject with fresh minds, readers will recognise that many of the conclusions which we have reached appear in the results of other studies. For example the (then) Accounting Standards Steering Committee's publication, *The Corporate Report*, which appeared in 1975, contains much that is in line with our own thinking. Where we believe that we have broken new ground is in considering management information needs along with those of external users and in the way in which we suggest that desirable information might be presented to external users of corporate reports.

CHAPTER 1

Background to Our Suggestions

1.1 Why should it be necessary to think again about the nature of corporate reporting? In this Chapter we explain where our deliberations led us.

1.2 We thought first of all about financial reporting itself (whether it be internal or external). What does it achieve? What is it intended to achieve? Surely the intention is to show what is actually happening to an entity, expressing the salient facts as far as practicable in financial terms. We decided, for reasons which we spell out more fully below and discuss in greater depth in Chapter 4, that frequently current external reporting does not fully achieve that intention. Accordingly we arrived at our first basic conclusion, namely that all financial reports ought to reflect economic reality. As a corollary, if financial reports do not reflect economic reality, they are deficient.

1.3 We then thought about the reasons for financial reports, which highlighted the importance of communication. In the context of corporate activity this normally means the communication of information about the functioning of a business entity by the lower echelons of the management structure to the higher and by the latter to the investors in the entity. This discussion document, though primarily concerned with information from management to investors, should, we decided, deal with both channels of communication. (By management we mean the top decision-taking level of an entity – the directors and senior managers. In investors we include anyone who has invested or intends to invest – shareholders, proprietors and long-term lenders.)

1.4 The investors in an entity (in the majority of cases the shareholders of a limited company) can involve themselves in the activities of that entity by:
(a) buying shares;
(b) selling shares;
(c) leaving their share ownership unchanged; or
(d) entering in some way into the management process.

Background to Our Suggestions

1.5 In order to decide what action is desirable on their part, investors will require information about the performance and the prospects of the entity and about the stewardship of the board of directors whom they have appointed to the entity.

1.6 The investors are the people who create the market for an entity's securities since it is they who buy and sell, or offer to buy and sell, those securities; and it should be in their interest generally that the market functions as efficiently as possible. We think that applies whether the matter is being considered on a local or on an international level. Reliable information about the economic reality of entities whose securities are being traded and a spread of that information to all the investors in the market should be important factors in the achievement of efficiency. Clearly, if some people have information about an entity that is withheld from other people, it is unlikely that a fair bargain will be struck and in such circumstances the efficiency of the market will suffer.

1.7 Those who have the responsibility of managing an entity (they are "insiders") cannot but know more about how it is performing and how it is likely to perform in the future than those with no day-to-day contact, whose knowledge is dependent upon what the insiders are willing to tell. Thus in many countries the law lays down the minimum amount of information which managements must communicate to investors and the time limits for doing so. The requirements of the law may or may not be supplemented by regulations of stock exchanges or other supervisory bodies.

1.8 We believe that the efficient operation of a market in securities requires the communication by managements to investors of information that will assist the latter in deciding which of the alternatives mentioned in paragraph 1.4 above they should adopt. We therefore considered what information the managements of well-run entities have available to them and compared it with what they pass on in the normal corporate report.

1.9 We have noted that some of the information that management have but do not normally communicate comes out into the open when management want something. For example, if management want additional capital, or if they want to defend or promote a takeover advance, disclosures such as are legally required for prospectuses are made. If management wish to defend their entity's share price, disclosures may be made to analysts that would not otherwise become public in the normal course of events. Without stimuli of these kinds most managements, understandably for fear of giving hostages to fortune, stick to what the existing regulations require.

Making Corporate Reports Valuable

1.10 Since, in most cases, the additional information is available within the entity anyway, little extra cost would be involved in giving it a wider airing. (Such extra costs as there are will largely be devoted to explanation and validation of the information that management want made known and want to be believed.) However, managements can presumably see specific benefits to the entity from wider disclosure only in the sort of cases envisaged above. Benefits to investors from additional information are difficult for anyone to quantify. (In some circumstances, such as the recent moves of newspaper groups from Fleet Street to Wapping, early disclosure of information by managements may act to the detriment of investors.) So, in cases other than those mentioned above, it seems unlikely that many managements will have any internally generated incentive to make additional disclosures.

1.11 We accept that the decisions which management have to take in running the entity are different from the decisions which investors have to take in relation to their investments. We also acknowledge that management have from time to time to resolve difficult conflicts in serving the interest of shareholders, not least in deciding whether or not to disclose information which, of course, becomes automatically available to a much wider constituency than shareholders. Nevertheless, from our consideration of the type of information which managements have (or should have), we find little that would not benefit the investors' decision-making process.

1.12 This leads to our second basic conclusion: the information which investors need in order to make proper decisions about their involvement with an entity is the same in kind, but not in volume, as the information which management need to run it.

1.13 However, our inquiries have shown that in well-run entities the annual corporate report is used very little, if at all, by managements as an aid to the proper conduct of their duties. This perhaps further explains why there has apparently been little demand from managements that corporate reporting should be changed. In any case, as we mentioned in paragraph 1.2 above, current financial reporting suffers from a number of deficiencies. It concentrates on the legal form of transactions more than on their economic substance and frequently does not reflect economic reality, it concentrates on the past rather than the future, it concentrates on cost rather than value and it leads to too much attention being paid to "profit" and not enough to wealth and changes in it.

Background to Our Suggestions

1.14 The two principal financial statements in a present-day corporate report are the profit and loss account and the balance sheet. But there is no consistent conceptual basis underlying the production of either statement. Indeed, some of the concepts used appear to defy normal understanding of financial affairs. As a result of the "form over substance" attitude, we are at present faced with trying to overcome an epidemic of off-balance sheet financing. As a result of ignoring the future, investors have to make their own projections from the information provided to them about the past – a not very satisfactory basis. And as a result of concentrating upon cost, it is impossible to judge alternative uses of an entity's resources or how much better off an entity really is than last time it reported.

1.15 Additionally, present-day financial statement packages seldom give any indication of the overall objectives of the entity; and even crucial information about its management and ownership is provided only on a limited scale.

1.16 There are two further criticisms of corporate reporting, which do not affect the financial statements but which are relevant to their usefulness to investors. The first is that corporate reports are not made public sufficiently speedily. The second is that the auditors' report, which is intended to add credibility to the management's representations, is insufficiently informative and often incomprehensible to non-auditors.

1.17 If our thinking outlined above is valid – and we believe it is – two courses were open to us in this study. We could, as most previous studies have done, suggest additions and amendments to the present regime. Alternatively, we could endeavour to restructure the corporate report in order to liberate it from the form which has become conventional and into which the present failings have become built. We decided that the second line of approach was the more profitable and worked out a structure which we believe should stimulate debate and research, as indicated in the Introduction. At the same time we took the opportunity to consider what improvements might be made to current reporting procedures in the meantime.

SUMMARY

1.18 *In this chapter we explained briefly what motivated us to undertake this study, namely a need to improve the communication of useful information by managements to*

Making Corporate Reports Valuable

investors. We identified the basic shortcomings of present-day financial reporting, – the adherence to legal form rather than economic substance, the use of cost rather than value, the concentration on the past rather than the future and the interest in "profit" rather than wealth.

1.19 *Given the efficient operation of a market in securities requires the communication by managements to investors of information that will assist the latter in deciding what action they should take in relation to the activities of their entities, we reached the following basic conclusions:*
   (a) financial reports ought to portray economic reality; and
   (b) the information which investors need is the same in kind, but not in volume, as the information which managements need to run their entities.

1.20 *These conclusions led us to decide that we should try to restructure corporate reports rather than only suggesting additions and amendments. But in the short term improvements can be made consistent with that long-term objective of major restructuring.*

CHAPTER 2

Corporate Governance and its Effects on Internal and External Reporting

2.1 Corporate reporting is concerned with the communication of information to those who have a right to receive it. Communicating information can be a costly process. The rights of certain parties to receive information and the duties of accountability placed upon entities are dependent upon the prevailing model of corporate governance, which is likely to change from time to time in response to social pressures. In this chapter we discuss the relevance to corporate reporting of contemporary views on corporate governance.

2.2 Three groupings are generally recognised as sharing the task of governance of companies and similar entities:
   (a) Regulatory authorities (Government, The Stock Exchange, etc).
   (b) The investors or other proprietors.
   (c) The management group, which can overlap with group (b) particularly in smaller entities.

2.3 There are four areas in which the above groupings have interests although they do not necessarily all have interests, or the same degree of interest, in all the areas:
   (i) The context and environment in which the entity operates.
   (ii) The entity's overall objectives.
   (iii) The strategy and tactics worked out to achieve those objectives.
   (iv) The results of (i), (ii) and (iii) above.

2.4 Although the entity, in the form which we are considering, has its individual legal *persona*, for practical purposes it is the board of directors (or equivalent) who are accountable for the activities of the entity. Their accountability is partly public and partly private. For example, the government will be interested in whether the entity pays its dues to society and whether it obeys the law. The directors are called upon to answer to government on such matters. They also have to account to the proprietorial group for the way in which they have exercised their stewardship of the

Making Corporate Reports Valuable

resources which the investors have entrusted to them. This accountability means that information has to be made available on behalf of the entity to those with a right to know.

2.5 The directors of an entity and its senior managers have a duty to ensure that it is operating efficiently and achieving its objectives. They should be using the entity's resources to the best of their abilities, and to do that they need information which will both enable them to monitor what is happening at the present and guide them on what should be done in the future.

2.6 Government as the rule-making authority can readily impose its requirements for information by demanding, for example, the completion periodically, or on an *ad hoc* basis, of statistical returns, such as those to the Department of Employment.

2.7 Management being the group involved in running the entity on a day-to-day basis can require the information appropriate to their requirements to be prepared for their decision-making purposes in whatever form they wish and whenever they need it.

2.8 This leaves the proprietorial grouping, which is not involved in the day-to-day management. Their involvement with the affairs of their entity is confined to the activities listed in paragraph 1.4 of Chapter 1. They will normally involve themselves in the management process – if they do so at all – only when something is going wrong. Understandably, because it is an easier course to adopt, the proprietors will often opt out by selling their investment rather than take a more interested position of how to resolve the difficulties the entity may be facing; this latter stance might include a change of some, or all, of the management.

2.9 The mechanism by which information is conveyed to the proprietors about the activities and status of their entities is external corporate reporting, which in many countries is the legal responsibility of the directors.

2.10 The same information that the directors are obliged to provide to the proprietors also goes on public record in many countries. In the United Kingdom this is achieved for limited companies by filing it with the Registrar of Companies, thus satisfying, in theory, a duty of accountability to a wider audience than just the proprietors.

2.11 There are other groups included in the wider audience who are interested in, but not actually involved with the governance of, entities and who may have a justifiable need for information. The identification of these groupings and their needs are discussed in Chapter 3.

Corporate Governance and its Effects on Reporting

SUMMARY

2.12 In this chapter we outlined the roles of regulatory authorities, proprietors and managements in business entities and their interactions with each other. We noted that they all have needs for information and indicated the means by which these needs are currently met.

CHAPTER 3

The Philosophy, Objectives and Scope of Internal and External Corporate Reporting

A. INTERNAL REPORTING

3.1 In Chapter 2 we referred to management's responsibility to employ efficiently the resources of their entity towards the objectives laid down and that they need information to assist them in doing so. The information which they need (and which we discuss later, in paragraph 3.11) is not confined to financial figures. "Management accounts", which are basically in figures, are useful for taking short-run operating decisions, identifying possible trouble spots and motivating management below board level, but directors and senior managers have more to do than that. They have to be constantly planning for the future within the environment in which the entity operates, and they have to take decisions about investment and disinvestment of the entity's resources. Obviously all managements of all entities do not have identical concerns or activities: much will depend on the nature and size of the entity and on the kind of business in which it is engaged. However, it can confidently be said that all managements need an information system which provides them with as much as possible of what they should know in order to carry out their duties within their individual entities. This system is the entity's internal reporting. We have reason to believe that nearly all well-run entities have internal reporting systems which will include various of the suggestions that we put forward later in this discussion document.

3.2 When planning for the future and deciding upon the investment or disinvestment of an entity's resources, we believe it to be essential that the information in front of boards of directors is as comprehensive as possible in order that they can discharge their responsibility to the proprietors effectively. It is the weekly, monthly, quarterly (whatever the period) management

The Philosophy, Objectives and Scope of Corporate Reporting

information package on which the fundamental decisions are made. For making such decisions the present published accounts are normally irrelevant.

3.3 Provided with an effective management information system, which, as indicated above, we understand most well-run companies to have, the directors and senior managers of an entity should be in possession of facts about their entity in an understandable form. What we suggest later (in Chapter 7) will, we believe, present the facts more fully and more effectively, which we hope will be welcome to all managements, especially as we believe that in successful companies they are normally progressive in their approach to potential improvements. We should like to think that a similar quality (but not quantity) of information could be made available to the investors in an entity, and we develop this theme further in section D of this chapter.

3.4 It must be remembered, in framing the financial information for inclusion in periodical internal reports, that not all directors and managers are equally numerate. Nevertheless, they bear the responsibility for the running of their entity and so need to understand what their information system is telling them. We believe that many of them find it helpful if the information on the financial position or outlook is presented in descriptive form rather than by columns of figures.

B. EXTERNAL USERS OF CORPORATE REPORTS

3.5 The 1975 *Corporate Report* defined external users as those having a reasonable right to information concerning the reporting entity arising from the public accountability of the entity. Its list of user groups was:
   (a) the equity investor group;
   (b) the loan creditor group;
   (c) the employee group;
   (d) the analyst-adviser group;
   (e) the business contact group;
   (f) the government; and
   (g) the public.

The 1975 *Report* recognised that while corporate reports should seek to satisfy as far as possible the information needs of these user groups it was impractical to suggest that all needs of all users could be entirely met by such general purpose reports.

3.6 In considering in 1988 the list of user groups, we believe that in

corporate reporting we should aim to communicate directly to only four of those groups listed above, namely:
(a) the equity investor group;
(b) the loan creditor group;
(c) the employee group; and
(d) the business contact group.

The last-mentioned group includes the ordinary creditors of an entity.

3.7 We agree with the 1975 *Corporate Report* that all the potential needs of the above users are unlikely to be met by general purpose reports. All that we can hope is that the suggestions which we make will improve reports sufficiently that there will be fewer needs left unmet.

3.8 We accept that the users of corporate reports in the above categories can cover the whole spectrum from those who are very knowledgeable in financial matters to those who tend to become bemused when faced with masses of figures. We believe that, so far as possible, reports should be framed in such a way that users can get what they want from them without having to turn for advice to an accountant, lawyer, economist or other specialist. Accordingly we shall be suggesting ways of presenting financial and other information which we hope will allow each category of user to obtain the picture he or she needs in the depth he or she can understand.

3.9 The reason that we do not include the analyst-adviser group in the list at 3.6 above is because we consider that this group does not have a *direct* right to information from the reporting entity. Analysts and advisers certainly use the external reports (along with other information) but they do so as agents for other groups. Logically, therefore, if we can suggest an information package satisfactory to those groups, we should be giving the analyst-adviser group what it needs. We should add here our opinion that managements should not make available to an analyst any information which they do not provide to the other external users at the same time.

3.10 We also considered that in corporate reporting we should not be seeking specifically to meet the information needs of government or of the public (other than in their capacities as investors, loan creditors or business contacts). For the reason given in paragraph 2.6 of Chapter 2 we did not think there would be a need for us, in considering the contents of corporate reports, to place any emphasis on seeking to meet the information needs of government, though if what we suggest meets some of those

The Philosophy, Objectives and Scope of Corporate Reporting

needs that will be a bonus. Regarding the public interest, we consider that this group's interests are covered by those of other groups. We could not identify an information need which could be attributed solely to the "general public". Furthermore, we consider that the public interest aspect should be taken care of by government as representatives of the public.

C. INTERNAL AND EXTERNAL INFORMATION NEEDS

3.11 We believe that the fundamental information needs of the four external user groups listed at 3.6 above, which external corporate reports should be able to contribute to meeting, are:
 (a) to know the corporate objectives of the entity (see Chapter 2, paragraph 2.3(ii)), and to be able to evaluate the performance against those objectives;
 (b) to know what the total wealth of the entity is now as compared with what it was at the time of the last corporate report and the reasons for the change;
 (c) to be able to judge where the entity is going in the future and whether it has the necessary financial and other resources to do so;
 (d) to have adequate information about the economic environment within which the entity has been operating and will be operating; and
 (e) to know the ownership and control of the entity itself and the experience and background of its directors and officials (including details of other directorships or official positions held).

3.12 As an expansion of our suggestion in paragraph 3.11 we believe that it will be helpful to all external users to know:
 (i) the entity's actual performance for the accounting period just past and how this compares with its previously published plan for that period;
 (ii) management's explanations of any significant variances between the two; and
 (iii) management's financial plan for the current and forward accounting periods and explanations of the major assumptions used in preparing it.

Such information will provide users not only with management's plans for the current period but also with information on how to judge the reliability of management's planning based on their

Making Corporate Reports Valuable

performance in the past period.

3.13 The investors' stewardship interests will be covered by paragraph 3.11 (a),(b) and (e) and paragraph 3.12(i) and (ii). Their interests in the future will be covered by paragraph 3.11 (c) and (d) and by (iii) of paragraph 3.12.

3.14 The suggestions in paragraph 3.11(a) to (e) are essentially a digest of the needs put forward in the 1975 *Corporate Report* for the equity investor group. In the summary of its Section on user needs, other requirements were added to this catalogue, which dealt with meeting the broader social needs of groups such as government and the public. We believe that our summary adequately covers the information needs of the four user groups which we identify at paragraph 3.6 above. We also believe that sub-paragraphs (a) to (d) cover the information needs of management.

D. EXTERNAL REPORTING

3.15 It is the responsibility of management to convey to those outside the entity with a right to know information about the entity that will meet the needs identified above.

3.16 Managements traditionally concentrate – and existing legal requirements in the UK support this – on presenting in the financial statements of the corporate report an account of their stewardship in the form of a record of past transactions; they do not seek to appraise and report what the entity's future performance may be. Yet businesses are not managed solely by an appraisal of past events. Managements have a responsibility for the future economic wellbeing of their entities and so must look to future expectations.

3.17 Investors in an entity should be interested in the stewardship of the management, but they should also be interested in future prospects. We believe that the corporate report ought to provide sufficient quantitative and qualitative information to help those users involved with the entity to make assumptions/predictions about its future performance. The corporate report should cover the past, present and future, providing some continuum and so reflecting the nature of the entity itself.

3.18 In giving expectations about the future, the management will be providing information which is not as firmly based on fact as that traditionally reported. The report will need to include financial planning information. Some of the perceived precision of the

The Philosophy, Objectives and Scope of Corporate Reporting

present report will therefore have to be sacrificed. However, as we believe that the new information will be of value to external users in deciding their future relationships with the entity, we should be willing to trade off some loss in the precision of the information in the report against an increase in its usefulness.

3.19 Under our suggestions management will be providing external users with information which at present is not disclosed except when there is a need for it to be made public. We appreciate the reluctance of managements to disclose more than they have to, but we think there are benefits to wider external disclosure that are not always realised:

(a) the more information that is available and the more widely spread the information is, the less will be the likelihood of insiders using information to their advantage;

(b) the amount and quality of the information available to the market will be enhanced, which should help the efficiency of the market; and should also improve the market's ability to value the entity concerned;

(c) the control of investors over management and their decisions will be improved;

(d) investors, while they will still have to make their own judgments about the past, present and future of the entity, will be provided with a firmer foundation on which to base those judgments; and

(e) the reputations of entities that take a forward-looking stance are normally enhanced.

3.20 A *caveat* has to be entered at this point: if too much of what is known to the directors and other insiders is made public, the company itself may suffer as a result of competitors and others making use of certain sensitive information. This would clearly be to the detriment of the investors. The subset of the internal information has therefore to be carefully tailored so that the maximum useful knowledge is available to the external groups with a right to such knowledge without giving so much that the entity and its owners will be prejudiced.

E. INDEPENDENT ASSESSMENT

3.21 The information released to external users is controlled by the management of an entity, who have particular established interests. One could be forgiven for expecting that, since the management of an entity are the agents of the proprietors for the purpose of running it, they would align their interests with those of their principals, but research has shown that this is not necessarily so. Most managements like the entities for which they are responsible to show to the outside world steady and increasing prosperity, so there may be temptation to use existing accounting conventions to this end. Additionally, as we shall show in the next chapter, the conventions themselves are not without flaw. A minority of managements, unfortunately, use various ploys to give a not-so-honest account, for one reason or another.

3.22 We therefore think that the financial information in external corporate reports should be attested at least annually by an independent assessor, who will express an unbiased opinion on the information reported. This, while not providing any sort of guarantee, does help to safeguard investors and creditors against significant errors or intentional deceptions. The assessor's role will be to examine and report on the reasonableness of the information presented. This contrasts with the present auditor's function of forming an opinion on financial representations by management which relate only to past events. Regarding future information, while the assessor cannot be certain about the figures in the plans, he can be expected to identify and examine the basis on which management's belief about the future is founded and how this is reflected in the financial statements, and to form an opinion on the reasonableness of what is shown.

3.23 We do not believe that the role of the independent assessor should extend to forming an opinion on the *efficiency* of management. We hope that what we are going to suggest by way of improved reporting will in most cases make inefficiencies more obvious. Nevertheless, there have been instances in the past, and there will undoubtedly be instances in the future, when inefficient managements have been able to operate for many years, to the detriment of the entities for which they were responsible. In such cases we can see the value of requiring what has been called in the past a "management audit" but we prefer to call a "management performance review". It might be carried out, for example, by a supervisory board (such as are found in certain European countries), and we consider it a matter which ought to be explored through a further research project. This kind of review is rarely encountered at present but could, if it became more widespread, have a beneficial effect for both management and shareholders and ultimately, no doubt, for the economy of the whole country. To require a management performance

The Philosophy, Objectives and Scope of Corporate Reporting

review must necessarily be the decision of the shareholders, or of the government in the public interest. That decision will be taken if one or other of these parties is satisfied that the benefits accruing will at least be commensurate with the costs.

SUMMARY

3.24   In this chapter we considered who the users of internal and external reports are and their needs.

3.25   We suggested that external reporting should aim to communicate directly to:
    (a) the equity investor group;   (c) the employee group; and
    (b) the loan creditor group;   (d) the business contact group;
and we thought that it should cover:
    (i) the performance of an entity towards meeting its objectives;
    (ii) the present total wealth of an entity compared with that at the previous reporting date and reasons for the change;
    (iii) likely future developments and the resources necessary to meet them;
    (iv) information about an entity's economic environment; and
    (v) information about the ownership and management of an entity.

3.26   We also suggested that managements, in order to manage properly, need to know items (i) to (iv) inclusive of the preceding paragraph.

3.27   What we suggested should be reported externally is more than is currently given and we explained that we believed there to be benefits in wider disclosure:
    (a) to prevent insiders using information to their advantage;
    (b) to help improve the efficiency of the market for an entity's securities;
    (c) to improve investors' control over their managements;
    (d) to give investors a firmer foundation on which to base their judgments; and
    (e) to enhance the reputation as forward-looking of the entities concerned.
We did, however, note that some sensitive information ought not to be made public.

3.28   We thought that a form of independent assessment of the external information provided would be necessary.

CHAPTER 4
Problems of Present-Day Accounts

A. CONCEPTUAL BASIS

4.1 The accounts which directors of companies are required to lay annually before the shareholders have evolved slowly over a long period of time and have almost invariably lagged behind the current needs of their users. Even the terminology has outgrown commonsense. For example, a balance sheet is no longer a sheet of the residual balances of undepreciated original cost which are carried forward in an entity's books and which mean something to an owner; rather it is a hotchpotch of costs, valuations and adjusted figures which indicate neither the worth of an entity as a whole nor the separate worths of its individual components. Similarly, a profit and loss account does not produce a realistic picture of profit or loss since many changes in an enterprise's financial wealth are omitted from the statement.

4.2 The trouble, as indicated in Chapter 1, is that the concepts upon which these statements are based are neither consistent nor logical and do not lead to a portrayal of economic reality.

B. THE OBJECTIVES OF THE ENTITY

4.3 Present-day corporate reports are not required to give any indication of the objectives of the entity. Any information given may well appear in extremely general terms either in the directors' report or in the chairman's statement (or an equivalent). Neither the chairman nor the board of directors are likely to be held to account for the failure of the entity to meet these vague objectives. Consequently external users frequently remain in the dark about the main aims of the entity and are unable to judge whether, and to what extent, they are being achieved.

C. PRESENT FINANCIAL POSITION AND PERFORMANCE

(a) Financial Position

4.4 The present balance sheet almost defies comprehension. Assets are shown at depreciated historical cost, at amounts representing current revaluations and at the results of revaluations of earlier periods (probably also depreciated); that is, there is no consistency whatsoever in valuation practice. The sum total of the assets, therefore, is meaningless and combining it with the liabilities to show the entity's financial position does not in practice achieve anything worthwhile. As we understand it, to arrive at a meaningful picture analysts have to dismantle the figures, include their own estimates and found their opinions on the result of that exercise.

(b) Performance

(i) Recognition of income

4.5 The depreciation of assets which are rising in value produces an adverse effect on the profit and loss account while the entity's wealth may actually have increased. The statutory (in UK) accounting principle that only realised gains can be brought into the profit and loss account has meant that a major part of a company's growth in wealth is not being reflected in that account but is either taken straight to reserves (which themselves are frequently meaningless to an external reader) or not accounted for at all. Unrealised losses on the other hand are brought to the profit and loss account and consequently an anomaly is created – only the downside is shown. Prudence in this case is a barrier to the truth, and the economic reality of the situation is not made apparent.

4.6 Present-day reporting practice by concentrating on realised gains leads to inconsistencies in the gain arising on the disposals of revalued assets – some entities measure the gain in terms of revalued book value, others in terms of original cost.

4.7 The profit and loss account suffers from a major deficiency in that its principal objective seems to be to produce one figure representing "profit" (or "loss"). This appears to lead preparers and users of the statement to what may be called a "bottom-line obsession", which means that they concentrate their attention on that figure and upon the earnings per share ratio derived from it. This distracts from all the various aspects of the entity's wealth and performance which are necessary for a proper understanding of the economic reality. This bottom-line obsession is believed to have led in some cases to a short-term view of income and the deferral of long-term expenditure since this may affect short-term profit (and the analysts' opinion of the entity's performance). Hence expenditure on research and development and on important maintenance may be delayed, and numerous arguments may occur between company and auditor over extraordinary (below the line) and exceptional (above the line) unusual items.

(ii) Components of Income

4.8 The present profit and loss account does not show the sources of the changes in a company's financial wealth.

4.9 A company's increase or reduction in financial wealth consists of six main components:
  (1) income/deficiency from ongoing operations;
  (2) income/deficiency from discontinuing operations;
  (3) income/deficiency from unusual events peripheral to the main line business of the enterprise;
  (4) gains/losses on the disposal of assets;
  (5) unrealised gains/losses on assets; and
  (6) gains/losses of a prior year not previously recognised.

Items (1) to (4) above figure in the contemporary profit and loss account. At present gains under item (5) can only be recognised when a company revalues assets and are taken direct to reserves whereas losses, as we have already noted, hit the profit and loss account. The adjustment of prior year items often means that expenses or income of a prior year never reach the profit and loss account at all since they are normally dealt with through the reserves. The present income statement is therefore defective in that all gains and losses recognised in an accounting period are not shown. For a full description of the all-inclusive change in a company's financial wealth, all the items would have to be disclosed.

(iii) Segmental Reporting

4.10 Additionally, there is little information on how the various segments of an entity are performing. The present disclosure is normally vague and unhelpful, giving inadequate information in terms of both geographical and industrial markets. It is impossible to attempt any meaningful analysis of the quality and quantity of an entity's future income and cash resources if the reader is not given information concerning the specific regions in which investment has taken place, the currencies involved, the types of products and services being supplied, the transfer prices used between segments and the investment in each sector.

(iv) Other Disclosures

4.11 Other disclosures, which are not usually currently made, would assist the user in evaluating the quality of reported change in wealth. It would be helpful to know the effect of a related party on an entity's transactions and about elements of expenditure, such as research and development or large advertising campaigns, which can be accelerated or deferred at management's discretion. Significant items on which it is difficult to place a reliable estimated figure should ideally be disclosed to enable the user to assess the probability of errors in management's estimates.

(c) Market Capitalisation

4.12 It is not the practice to disclose the value that the market places on an entity's issued capital. Accordingly there is nothing to concentrate the minds of readers of corporate reports on the difference between that figure and the figure shown in the balance sheet for shareholders' funds. We feel that there could be definite advantages in being able easily to make the comparison and to seek explanations of the difference. This idea is developed later.

(d) What is the Entity?

4.13 So far we have simply discussed the financial position and performance of an individual entity. Users of financial statements require to know the economic power of a group of entities. This leads to two questions:
(1) What is the group?
and
(2) How shall we account for the assets and liabilities under the control of a central management?
The present-day problems which arise from these questions are discussed below.

(e) Consolidated Financial Statements

(i) Business Combinations

4.14 At present, two methods are allowed for business combinations:
(1) acquisition accounting where the consideration is valued at its market value, ie when shares are offered the market value

of these shares is regarded as the purchase price (or part of it if cash is also involved); and

(2) merger accounting where shares given as the consideration are valued in relation to their nominal value.

4.15 As shares and cash are used interchangeably in many business combinations it is difficult to rationalise the use of nominal value in merger (as opposed to acquisition) accounting, that is, the indefensible method of valuing net assets of an acquired company in relation to the nominal value of the shares offered. We do not believe that the resultant financial statement shows a true and fair view and we think that directors are wrong to suggest, and auditors to agree, that it does.

4.16 In addition, the results as shown in the profit and loss accounts under the two methods are completely different. This can be confusing to users of the accounts, who will be unable to judge either the real quantity or the quality of the increase in wealth resulting from the combination. Comparison of results year by year or with those of similar entities becomes virtually impossible.

(ii) Goodwill

4.17 A similar problem arises with goodwill created at the time of acquisition. At present, accounting standards prefer that goodwill be written off immediately against reserves although they accept that companies can still amortise goodwill through the profit and loss account. This divided opinion results in inconsistency in accounting treatment. Yet acquired goodwill of this nature can often be sold; in that sense goodwill has value and should only be written off as appropriate. Clearly where no value exists, goodwill should be written off immediately. However, the present practice of removing it totally from the balance sheet as soon as possible can mean that an asset, albeit intangible, which an entity really possesses is not shown as being in its possession. Consequently the treatment can result in shareholders' funds being reported as drastically reduced – a situation far removed from reality. Moreover, future borrowing powers may be affected.

(iii) The Entities in the Group

4.18 Apart from the valuation of assets of the group a further problem is the composition of the group. We have witnessed in recent years the growth of off-balance sheet dependent entities which are not subsidiaries in terms of the existing law but which have similar characteristics. They have been used to hide certain assets and borrowings which would otherwise have figured in the

Problems of Present-Day Accounts

accounts of group companies. So the law is being used to conceal the truth of the control exercised over those assets and liabilities. Other forms of off-balance sheet accounting are also used to hide the real assets and liabilities of a company or group. In such cases financial statements are defective in that the economic reality of the group's activities and status is hidden from the reader.

4.19 A further problem exists in the inclusion of associated companies in group accounts. In practice it is found that there are sometimes disputes between so-called associates and the entity preparing to equity account for its share in the associates as to whether the former are subject to significant influence exerted by the latter. To include profit from an implacably hostile investee company does not display the actual control or influence over that company – this is not accounting, it is merely arithmetic; the result does not display the reality of the relationship between the companies.

(f) Comprehensibility

4.20 For the reasons outlined above, present-day financial statements are often almost incomprehensible to anyone other than their preparers. This incomprehensibility is compounded by users' lack of full understanding of the concepts employed and the unclear terminology appearing in the statements themselves. Terms such as "profit", "reserves", "goodwill", "current assets", "depreciation" and the like, which may be words in ordinary use but which in accounting have specialised meanings (sometimes more than one for each word), can be misleading to readers. Even the present format of financial statements is not particularly clear to anyone who is not an accountant or mathematician and the way in which the figures balance and tie in with each other can give an impression of precision and accuracy that has never been intended. While we accept that it is not easy to make financial statements simple, they are supposed to help their readers: in their present form they fall short of that objective.

D. FUTURE FINANCIAL POSITION AND PERFORMANCE

4.21 Present-day financial statements offer little in the way of an evaluation of the future: the balance sheet does not enable the user to judge what alternative uses could be made of the portfolio of assets at the entity's disposal; valuation practices adopted do

Making Corporate Reports Valuable

not show the financial wealth at an entity's command.

4.22 Additionally, very little information is given concerning the entity's future prospects, since no budgets or forward plans are presented unless the entity is seeking to obtain additional capital. All an external user will receive will be (what are frequently anodyne) comments in the directors' report or chairman's statement. The future cash flow of an entity has to be estimated by the user. He is totally cut off from the information which management should regard as vital to the direction of the entity. The external user therefore has little in a corporate report to help him form a view on the entity's potential future performance and financial position.

E. ECONOMIC ENVIRONMENT

4.23 Except for very general comments in chairmen's reports, external users receive little information from managements about the environment within which the entity is operating. They have to do their own research (if they have the time and knowledge) into the state of the market in which the entity deals, its share of the market, the performances of its competitors and so on. Since management must have such information in order to manage properly, it seems unfortunate that the knowledge is not shared with the external users.

F. OWNERSHIP, MANAGEMENT AND STAFF

4.24 There is little information given at present in corporate reports about those who manage the entity. Many of the directors will be unknown to external users. No information is given about their past experience, other directorships held or even their suitability for the post they hold. External report users are asked to take on trust the competence of management. Past experience has shown that in some cases this is not a good basis for judging whether to invest in, or advance money to, a business.

4.25 Similarly, the information currently given on the staffing of an entity is very meagre and we think that it could be improved.

G. AUDIT

4.26 Although the audit report normally takes up very little space in a present-day corporate report, this in no way reflects the amount of work undertaken to arrive at it or the importance of the audit to the figures presented. Unfortunately there is no evidence to show that the nature of an audit is fully understood by all those interested in financial statements.

4.27 There are many misconceptions about the present auditor's role, such as:
  (a) the auditor checks each transaction;
  (b) the auditor judges the wisdom and legality of each transaction;
  (c) the auditor certifies the accounts for the purpose of investment decisions;
  (d) the auditor certifies the accounts as being correct; and
  (e) the auditor agrees that a company's results can be shown as a single number.

4.28 The present audit report does not help to clarify the situation. It is exceedingly cryptic, written in auditor's jargon and probably incomprehensible to those (and especially overseas readers) who are not or have not been auditors themselves.

4.29 How many readers realise that there is no unique "true and fair view"; and that an unqualified audit report does not mean that there is no fraud or error, only that the auditor is reasonably confident that no material misstatement (eg significant fraud or error) exists in the financial statements? How many readers can distinguish between the meaning of a "subject to" qualified report and that of an "except for" one? We suspect that, whatever is said in the current short-form report many readers will think that the appearance of the auditor's name in relation to the financial information published must mean that it is all right. If true, this is not a healthy state of affairs.

SUMMARY

4.30 *In this Chapter we suggested a number of deficiencies in present-day financial statements. We criticised the present balance sheet for being virtually meaningless and the present profit and loss account for not recognising all the gains or losses of a financial period. We were concerned that financial reports do not portray economic reality.*

Making Corporate Reports Valuable

4.31 We identified areas where either insufficient or misleading information is given, for example in relation to:
 (a) business segments;
 (b) business combinations;
 (c) goodwill; and
 (d) the entities within a group;
and we criticised lack of information on:
 (e) an entity's objectives;
 (f) future financial position and performance;
 (g) the economic environment; and
 (h) ownership, management and staff.

4.32 We suggested current misconceptions about the auditor's role and deficiencies in the present style of reporting.

CHAPTER 5

Some Possible Solutions

INTRODUCTION

5.1 In Chapter 4 we identified the principal problems which we have met in present-day accounting and reporting. In this chapter we shall put forward our ideas on how these problems may be resolved, with an eye mainly to the short and medium terms. We shall also refer briefly to further suggestions for the improvement of the corporate report; these will be developed in our suggested long-term strategy for internal and external reporting in Chapter 7.

5.2 We appreciate that our suggestions here can be used to ameliorate some of the causes of dissatisfaction under the existing conventions, and we hope that they will. We do not, however, believe that a "patching up" job is the ideal solution.

A. CONCEPTUAL BASIS

5.3 We believe that the total wealth of an entity and the changes in it from period to period are what should be of major importance to managements and to investors. By publishing the statements suggested for the use of management in Chapter 7, entities would eliminate most of the conceptual problems which we have identified in present-day financial statements. This, however, is a longer-term objective.

B. OBJECTIVES OF THE ENTITY

5.4 In Chapters 2 and 3 we noted management's need to have before them the objectives of the entity, and we suggested that external user groups would wish to judge the effectiveness of the entity in achieving those objectives. Neither of the requirements can be adequately met unless the management formally draw up a Statement of Corporate Objectives; it should be reviewed by the board on a regular basis.

5.5 This statement, or an appropriate summary of it, should be contained in every corporate report issued.

C. PRESENT FINANCIAL POSITION AND PERFORMANCE

5.6 **(a) Financial Position**

In the short run the problem of the heterogeneous nature of assets shown in contemporary balance sheets could be partially overcome by requiring regular revaluations. We would suggest that all fixed assets be revalued at least every five years.

5.7 The longer-term aim, in our view, should be to draw up a statement of assets and liabilities annually on a value basis, with a view to displaying as fairly as possible the financial wealth of the entity at each accounting date. Our preference, where practicable, is for net realisable values, and we give our reasons for this in Chapter 6. We believe that it would help the introduction of our suggested reporting package (in Chapter 7) if the revaluations mentioned in the preceding paragraph were at net realisable values at any rate for land and buildings (the amounts for which are normally not difficult to ascertain).

5.8 Under this suggested regime managements' wisdom in continuing to employ certain assets would be more apparent and the valuation policy would give a truer presentation of the enterprise's command over economic resources and more fairly reflect the change from year to year.

(b) Performance

(i) Recognition of income

5.9 The adoption of a value basis of accounting would remove many of the difficulties which we have identified in relation to the present profit and loss account. It would obviate the need for a depreciation charge when assets were gaining in value, although assets which were losing value would still need to be written down to their current value. There will be those who think that revenue should bear a charge for the consumption of assets used in earning it: this would mean, under our suggestion, the results of the period including the write-up for any increase in the worth of an asset and a write-down to provide for consumption. This makes sense if one accepts the matching concept of measuring profit, but it is rather cumbersome. If the comparison of financial wealth from period to period is accepted as the basis for judging results, we are of the opinion that the double step is unnecessary.

5.10 Because it militates against economic reality, we should like to see the dropping from UK company law of the emphasis on

Some Possible Solutions

"prudence" (conservatism). What is required is a balanced view which is neither overly optimistic nor overly pessimistic. For example, there should be no prohibition of bringing unrealised gains into the profit and loss account.

5.11 A proper understanding of the state of an entity's liquidity over a period (cash flow position) and an appreciation of how and why its net quantifiable assets (financial wealth) position has altered during a financial period are, we believe, of far more practical use to managements than a statement showing how much "profit" the company has made. This being so, the same information should be more helpful to other users of financial statements, and we should like to see that information taking the place of the "bottom line" in the importance accorded by users. We think that it would help to alleviate the disadvantages of the short-termism suggested in Chapter 4.

(ii) Components of income

5.12 We believe that information on growth in a company's wealth, along the lines indicated in paragraph 4.9 of Chapter 4, should be given. It could be done immediately by adding a further statement to the statutorily required ones bringing together the various sources of gain, whether realised or unrealised. In the longer term we should like to see the Operations Statement and the Changes in Wealth Statement suggested in Chapter 7 taking care of this information.

(iii) Segmental reporting

5.13 Although it seems probable that a call for additional segmental information will not be welcomed by some potential providers, we believe that disclosure should be made beyond what is at present required and provided. We accept that there will be concern lest too much assistance is given to competitors or, in some cases, to governments or trade unions. However, secrecy can be carried too far (as some City financial and political scandals have shown) and fears about disclosing can sometimes be more figments of the imagination than realities. Provided that everyone gives information in the same measure economic forces should operate to produce economically desirable results. We recognise, however, that it is unreasonable and unrealistic to expect total disclosure until there is worldwide acceptance of the need, so that entities disclosing in one country would not be at a disadvantage with the entities not required to do so in another.

5.14 We therefore believe that information relating to the increase or decrease in wealth of an entity should be disclosed to external

Making Corporate Reports Valuable

users in sufficient detail to allow such users to judge where (in the world, in the sales mix, in the group or wherever) the material gains or losses are occurring and to foresee what may happen in these segments in the future. The nature of the segments will obviously be determined by the nature, size, geographical spread, etc of the entity concerned.

5.15 We develop our own thinking on segmental reporting in the future in Chapter 7.

(iv) Related party transactions

5.16 We considered the problem of related parties in the group context in Chapter 4, and shall do so again later in this chapter. In almost all the cases of fraud or misconduct which Department of Trade Inspectors have considered during the past twenty-five years related parties have played a role. It is so easy to use them to hide the effects of transactions from those who do not realise the relationship. We therefore recommend that it should be a requirement for all reporting entities to identify related parties in their corporate reports, so far as they are known, and to disclose the effects of all significant transactions in which they were involved. The disclosure should be in sufficient detail that an outsider would be aware of the actual situation of the parties concerned. We believe that the law should be changed as soon as possible to make this compulsory, on the pain of stiff penalties.

(v) Other disclosures

5.17 Because of the inherent uncertainties of life, and particularly in business situations, we suggest that it would be desirable for management to disclose in each corporate report the areas of their accounting which are particularly subject to uncertainty and the boundaries of that uncertainty. It would be useful to know, in the case of significant amounts that have had to be estimated, the possible margin of error which the management foresee. Expenditure that can be delayed or brought forward (possibly with the intent of smoothing income from one period to another) should also be disclosed.

5.18 We also believe there should be a statement on relative innovation where the amounts are sufficiently significant so that management and investors are aware of the stance that the company is adopting in relation to innovation. By relative we mean:

(a) The proportion of production that is new and conceived internally or self-generated.
(b) How this compares to competitive entities.

Some Possible Solutions

5.19　This does not entail the disclosure of details about the nature of what has been thought up during, say, the last two years, only a quantification. Additionally, there should be some information illustrating the effectiveness (and the lead time) of research and development where those are important, and this information should be linked to that on relative innovation.

(c) Market Capitalisation

5.20　However an entity's identifiable assets and liabilities are measured and reported, the result will never signify the real worth of the entity. (The reason for this is considered in Chapter 7, paragraph 7.13.) In theory, the real worth can be computed only by calculating the present value of all the future cash flows to the entity. While we are aware of instances where that has been done, the results are likely to be so imprecise and the degree of subjectivity so high that we cannot recommend it as a figure which ought to be reported to investors and other external users of financial information. However, we think that research and experimentation in this area are highly desirable.

5.21　We believe it to be desirable that not only external users but management themselves should be aware of the approximate value of the unidentifiable or unmeasurable net "assets" from which an entity benefits. They form part of the entity's market capitalisation. In the long term we should like to see a set of financial statements which bring this out, but in the meantime we suggest that it would be helpful if managements disclosed the market capitalisation figure. This, to some extent, is an external measurement of the entity's financial wealth, even though the market prices are affected by environmental factors such as wars, civil disturbances, general stock market sentiment, industry strikes, possible takeovers and other matters over which management may have no control. It would also be helpful if management would comment on the difference between the market valuation and the disclosed financial wealth (by whatever means that may be arrived at).

(d) Consolidated Financial Statements

5.22　In the long term, whether acquisition accounting or merger accounting is used we believe that all assets should be revalued at net realisable values for the purposes of the consolidated accounts; this would avoid the indefensible method of valuing net assets of an acquired company in relation to the nominal value of

Making Corporate Reports Valuable

the shares offered in a merger. In the short term, however, one possible solution would be to require the fullest disclosure of what has been done when merger accounting has been used and a comparison of what the result would have been using the acquisition method.

5.23 We think that the income statement for the year during which a business combination takes place should incorporate the combined results for the whole period regardless of whether acquisition or merger accounting is used. We believe that that would be helpful in comparing past years with the current year and the current year with plans for the future, whichever method has been used. We also feel that users should be able to see what part of the results related to the pre-combination period and was therefore (presumably) taken into account in fixing the purchase price of the acquired company.

5.24 We dislike the policy used by some companies of making excessive provisions for reorganisation expenses when businesses combine and acquisition accounting is used. These charges simply add to the goodwill arising on a combination, which present day practice tends to write off to reserves. We suspect that on many occasions companies are seeking to smooth their profits (or show steeply rising profits) by the use of these provisions and writing off against them future losses unanticipated at the time of the combination or even writing back the excess provision in "bad years". We therefore believe that reorganisation provisions should be written off to the profit and loss account as an unusual item in the year of combination.

5.25 We find the term "goodwill" to be misleading in all accounts. The concept arises most commonly on consolidation, and we think its nature in that (and any other) circumstance needs to be carefully explained in a note. Our view is that this asset should not be written off unless management are clear that its value has been lost (and the auditors agree). If our proposals for presentation along the lines suggested in Chapter 7 are accepted, the problem should be taken care of and the position be more comprehensible to users of the financial statements.

(e) Associated Companies

5.26 As indicated in Chapter 4, associated companies can give rise to manipulation of the figures currently disclosed in the financial statements. The key element in each case is whether the consolidating company actually has a degree of influence over the

Some Possible Solutions

activities of the other. We believe that the management of the former should obtain confirmation or denial from the latter that significant influence exists, and the respective auditors form a judgment as to the accuracy of the individual managements' understandings of the position.

5.27 As regards the investing company's accounts, if no significant influence is held in the other entity, only dividends should be shown and the investee holding should be shown simply as an investment in the balance sheet and not equity accounted (in accordance with our preference, already indicated, we should like it to be shown at market value).

(f) Off-Balance Sheet Financing and Window Dressing

5.28 The ploy of using non-subsidiary dependent companies as a means of off-balance sheet financing was also referred to in Chapter 4. There are, in addition, other legal methods of removing assets and liabilities from an entity's balance sheet. We believe that control (rather than legal ownership) over the activities of another entity, so that both work as one economic unit, should be the dominating factor in deciding whether or not to consolidate, and that economic substance should always prevail over legal form in the presentation of a company's state of affairs and results. This would bring the accounting rules in this country into line with those in some other parts of the world. There should be a note, however, setting out clearly what the legal position is and what effect it would have if anything happened to trigger off legal action.

5.29 Window dressing, which is always intended to mislead, should be outlawed. We take the view that the remedy of providing a note explaining the real position is insufficient and the accounts should invariably be adjusted. The adjustment should be the subject of a note explaining what has been done.

5.30 Clearly the elimination of both undesirable practices will place a responsibility on auditors but since, in our view, both are a distortion of a true and fair view, we believe the responsibility to be there already.

(g) Comprehensibility

5.31 While in the long term we should like to see a change in the way financial information is presented, we think that improvements can be made even with the conventional form of financial statements.

5.32 To present such statements in a virtually incomprehensible fashion is about as sensible as presenting the news in Arabic to the British public. A few people will understand what it is all about but the majority will be completely lost. We do not subscribe to the view sometimes advanced that accounts need to be translated for the lay user: we believe that they should be comprehensible to a reasonable person. (This applies particularly in the UK where the privatisation of state-owned entities has led to an increasing number of individual shareholders.)

5.33 We think that technical jargon (or "terms of art") should be avoided throughout internal and external reports so far as possible. If, in rare instances, there is no obvious alternative to a technical term, we should like to see it defined.

5.34 We also support for directors and investors a full statement of Accounting Policies (along present lines) but avoiding technical jargon. A clear explanation of the Accounting Standards applicable to the particular set of financial statements might also be helpful to external users.

5.35 We believe that external users of financial statements tend to make certain assumptions about the figures if nothing is said elsewhere in the corporate report. For example, the systems of control of the business by management are satisfactory, and there has been no significant fraudulent or illegal activity. On the latter point we do not feel qualified to suggest whether or not managements should have a responsibility to disclose to the investors the consequences of any significant fraud, illegality or major incompetence that comes to light. This is a difficult and complicated subject which we feel could form the basis of a useful research project.

5.36 There is also likely to be the assumption that everything important is disclosed. It would probably be helpful to users to have some knowledge of how management and the auditors decide whether a matter is material because it would provide some indication of the basis for that assumption and would also suggest the extent to which figures might not be strictly accurate. However, we accept that the concept of materiality is a very difficult one to pin down: it could almost be said that there is a mystical aspect to it. Accordingly, although intuitively we should like to see the information given in corporate reports, we suspect that what could be given at the present time might not prove very useful. This is another area where we should like to see research and experimentation taking place.

Some Possible Solutions

D. FUTURE FINANCIAL POSITION AND PERFORMANCE

5.37   That existing and potential investors need to form a view about the future of their investment is not in question. As we have seen, they get little assistance from financial statements at present.

5.38   Management are much more concerned about the future than the past. From this point of view, they almost never use their own published accounts when taking policy decisions (though they will think about the impact on the accounts of the decisions they take). We suggest that the future-orientated material which managements employ in planning the business should, up to a point, be available to the shareholders as well.

5.39   We expect that the changeover to publishing future-orientated material will be a longer-term process than some of the other improvements which we are suggesting. We shall accordingly expand our ideas about what might be available to management and what to investors in Chapter 7.

5.40   Expected income of the future does not give the full picture of possible future dividends. We think that it should be made clear under the existing regime how much of the "reserves" is available for distribution. We have placed "reserves" in inverted commas because, as mentioned in Chapter 4, it is not a concept that is fully understood and we believe clarification would be helpful to accounts users.

E. ECONOMIC ENVIRONMENT

5.41   Management should have before them information about important aspects of the economic environment within which the entity operates, and we can see no reason why it cannot also be made available to investors. The sort of information which we think management have and most of which could be published in the corporate report, if of sufficient significance, is discussed in the following paragraphs.

(a) The Market Place

5.42   Every entity requires to have information on various aspects of its market. That information would come mainly from outside the entity. The major divisions we would suggest are the following:

Making Corporate Reports Valuable

- (i) The size of the market(s) – there would need to be a clear definition of "the market", possibly coming from any relevant trade association in order that, in published information, like is being compared to like.
- (ii) The strength of the market(s) and the position of demand and supply.
- (iii) Market share, ie what proportion of the relevant markets, as defined under (i) above, managements think their own entities enjoy.
- (iv) Economic facts likely to affect the market(s) – these would include the review of possible parity changes as well as an assessment of the actual health of the market in local currency terms.
- (v) Political factors likely to affect the market(s).
- (vi) What major competitors are doing.

5.43 Obviously, the same sort of segmentalisation that was discussed earlier – subject to the same caveats and particularly to the danger of an excessive volume of information – needs equally to be applied here. If an entity is a multi-product entity, at management level the market for each of the main types of product would have to be considered, and the market would have to be split appropriately.

(b) Comparative Operational Statistics

5.44 We think there should be information on comparative operational statistics, eg comparing the operational statistics of the entity under consideration with information culled from similar statements by its competitors or other entities in similar markets.

F. OWNERSHIP AND MANAGEMENT

5.45 *The Corporate Report* suggested that accounts users need to know "the ownership and control of the entity" and to be able to assess "the experience and background of company directors and officials including details of other directorships or official positions". We agree. Our suggestions above on related parties, together with existing requirements to disclose ultimate parent, major shareholdings, etc help, but we think there should be a considerable increase in the details currently required by law about directors and senior managers. A statutory requirement for

Some Possible Solutions

each entity to publish in its report details of the directors' and senior managers' past and present directorships would undoubtedly assist those who invest in or lend to an entity to judge whether those who control its affairs are fit and proper people to do so.

5.46 As well as having insufficient background information on directors and managers, investors and other external users are frequently unaware of where the responsibility for the financial statements lies. As part of the basic information which an entity should publish we think that there should be a statement clarifying the responsibilities of the directors for preparation of the financial statements to a stated standard, and for proper internal controls and adequate accounting records. This should include an explanation of the duties of the company's audit committee (if any – or a statement to that effect if none) which is usually, but not always, made up of directors. The statement should then go on to explain the responsibilities of the auditors (independent assessors).

G. STAFF RESOURCES

5.47 Although the staff of an entity are not an asset in the sense that we have defined that term (see "Vocabulary"), it is undeniable that the contribution that the personnel make to an entity's wellbeing is an important factor which management and outside users of corporate reports need to know about.

5.48 For the purposes of management, there should be a plan to meet the short- and long-term staff requirements determined for each discipline and particularly for staff whose salaries are in the brackets which currently have to be reported in the annual accounts. Combined with an annual staff assessment and appraisal system which shows, *inter alia*, short- and long-term promotion potential for each staff member within the groups described above, excesses or shortages at each of these levels over the periods reviewed would be established. Promotion opportunities or gaps, training and recruitment requirements would be identified and the feasibility of successfully meeting the planned staff levels highlighted. At least a short explanation of how these matters might affect the future and how management plan to deal with them could be provided to investors.

5.49 In the short term we do not think very much more can be done for external users, although it would be satisfactory if the personnel's contribution to the difference between an entity's market capitalisation and its financial wealth could be arrived at in some way. There have been many research papers on the topic of "human asset accounting" but it must be said that the record of trying to bring the "human asset" into published financial statements has, after twenty years of trying, been rather unsatisfactory. Very few entities have adopted the concept and even fewer have sustained their interest over any substantial period.

5.50 In the light of the current situation, we think that there should be a major research project on the best way of reporting to management and investors on the worth of personnel.

H. AUDIT (INDEPENDENT ASSESSMENT)

(a) The Report

5.51 There will be implications for independent assessors in the suggestions we shall be making for long-term improvements in corporate reporting. We shall mention these briefly at the appropriate stage. In the short term we believe that the auditor's report should be made more understandable, written in plain language and should avoid the use of everyday terms intended to have special significance such as "except for" or "subject to". It should be in long rather than short form.

5.52 It should explain clearly the auditor's responsibilities, the way in which audits are conducted, the limitations of the audit (eg the nature of sampling) and the responsibility of management for the financial statements and for internal control. The fact that the audit report is intended to give reasonable assurance, but not a guarantee, that a true and fair view is shown in financial statements should also be stated.

5.53 Auditors should be more prepared to highlight significant features of a company's accounts and assist the reader in interpreting the financial statements by guiding him to the salient parts of these statements, for example by pointing out particular assumptions that have been made by management and accepted by the auditor. Similarly, when qualifying a set of financial statements, the auditor should spell out *clearly* the problem in such a way that the reader will be able to judge the effect. The auditor's report would then be longer but would be more informative and the auditor would be providing an additional service for those reading the accounts. For this reason we believe that the auditor's report should immediately precede the financial statements rather than be tucked away in some later part of the annual report.

(b) Audit Committees

5.54 Audit committees currently form a very useful liaison between the directors and the auditors. They provide an opportunity for difficulties to be openly discussed, especially at an early stage.

5.55 The foreseen expansion of the scope of the independent assessor's work referred to above will, we believe, mean a greater use of audit committees to consider more issues and to hear the concern of the assessor on particular topics, including corporate plans and policies.

5.56 The introduction and/or further development of audit committees, preferably drawn from the non-executive directors, should be encouraged for all companies. This evolution of their function and status should make them an integral part of the corporate control.

SUMMARY

5.57 *In this chapter we have tried to suggest ways in which the defects identified in Chapter 4 might be repaired within a reasonably short space of time. We indicated that we do not consider a "patching up" ideal but rather a step towards a new and better package.*

5.58 *We have suggested new or improved disclosures to meet the criticisms summarised in paragraph 4.31 of Chapter 4, and we have outlined how we would deal with the conceptual problems of present-day accounts. In brief we suggest that:*

(a) fixed assets are revalued on a regular basis and in due course market value (net realisable value) should be used for all assets and liabilities;

(b) write-down of assets is purely on the basis of loss in value;

(c) unrealised gains (disclosed as being unrealised) are reflected in increases in financial wealth;

(d) the primacy of the true and fair view is re-established and that greater emphasis should be placed on ensuring that accounts are based less on "rules" and more on economic reality;

(e) all components of the changes in financial wealth are revealed in a single statement; and

Making Corporate Reports Valuable

      (f)   disclosure is given of future plans and potential liabilities or gains.

5.59 In addition we have indicated what we think might be done in disclosing information about:
      (a)   transactions with related parties;
      (b)   areas of uncertainty, major estimated figures and discretionary items;
      (c)   relative innovation and research and development activity;
      (d)   associated companies;
      (e)   off-balance sheet financing and window dressing; and
      (f)   comparative operational statistics.

5.60 We have also made suggestions on how the information in corporate reports could be made more comprehensible to external users.

5.61 We have indicated how we think the present auditor's report could be improved and have advocated more use of audit committees.

CHAPTER 6

Valuation of Assets and Liabilities

INTRODUCTION

6.1 Up to this stage in our discussion document the suggestions that we have made could be adopted within a reasonably short time span if, after debate, they were found acceptable. From this point onwards, we look forward to a longer period of research, discussion and experimentation. So, in this chapter we discuss the problem of placing valuations on assets and liabilities of entities in the corporate report. We advocate the use of net realisable values for this purpose in most cases.

A. ASSET VALUATION METHODS AVAILABLE

6.2 For many years there have been debates about the monetary values which should be shown in accounts to represent assets and liabilities. The main methods which have been advocated are historical cost (HC), current replacement cost (RC), current net realisable values (NRV) and economic values. Each has its strengths, and each its weaknesses.

6.3 There have also been a number of combination methods suggested. The idea of showing the value of an asset to the firm was adopted in SSAP16, and this involved choosing, in defined circumstances, among the last three of the four methods above. It is possible that this method was too complicated to enjoy general acceptance.

6.4 In trying to decide which method to use, we have considered the main criteria to be additivity and reality. By additivity, we mean that all the numbers in a statement, when added together, should have a sum which has the same meaning as each of the numbers taken on its own. The old adage about adding apples and oranges is applicable here. By reality, we mean that the numbers in the account should resemble, as closely as practicality permits, one or more important economic facts – not conjectures, about which reasonable and skilled people might differ widely, but facts, about which the range of skilled opinion would be limited.

6.5 The historical cost method has already been criticised in earlier chapters. It fails the test of additivity completely because pounds sterling (or American dollars or whatever) of different dates and therefore different values (apples and oranges) are being added together. It may also be said to fail the test of reality in the sense that the amount which was paid for an asset at a past date is not, now, an important economic fact. It is an historical fact, of course; but that is a different matter.

6.6 The current replacement cost was the main method advocated during the debates leading to SSAP16. This method passes both tests. The sum of the replacement costs will represent the total cost which would be incurred if the entity had to re-equip itself at the accounting date, with substantially identical assets. The reality of these numbers is also clear. Most corporate managements keep themselves informed of new developments in their respective fields, and take account of up-to-date prices in judging whether a new project should be undertaken. There are complex practical problems in doing this, especially when technology changes or if an asset is never going to be replaced, as the history of the CCA debate has sufficiently illustrated. But the concept is valid in its own right.

6.7 The present value of the cash flows which will arise from an asset are quite clearly the main theoretical basis for the capital investment appraisal systems in general use. Economists and engineers agree with financial analysts that the method is the correct one for the appraisal for future use. The concept also passes the additivity test. Unfortunately, the subjectivity and uncertainty involved in its calculation mean that it cannot pass the reality test. The arguments which take place in the capital investment review committees of major entities are largely devoted to reviewing the assumptions upon which these cash flow streams are based. The conclusion, to proceed or not, is a perfectly legitimate conclusion when reached by management within an enterprise in these particular circumstances. But applied to an entity as a whole, particularly a large group, the concept would be costly, and the high level of uncertainty would militate against its ready acceptance.

6.8 The remaining method of asset valuation is current net realisable values. These are the values which the assets could be sold for, if disposed of in an orderly fashion, near the time of the account. As these numbers could be looked upon as a "price list" for an orderly sale, they pass the additivity test. All the numbers are current selling prices, and their total is the amount the firm would get for the whole batch.

Valuation of Assets and Liabilities

6.9 The net realisable value method also passes the reality test, as the value which the assets could be expected to realise is an important economic fact. For many assets the NRV can be found quite easily. It appears now in balance sheets for some investments, stock written down from cost and some properties. It must be said, however, that there are some assets which are not so easy to sell as those just mentioned. This can arise especially in the case of specialised plant and machinery, which might, in extreme cases, be quite impossible to dispose of. The value in exchange of such items may be nil, or even negative. Their value arises, of course, from the fact that they are going to be used in the business for some future period, and there is an expectation that this usage will be profitable. The assets themselves are worthless but, when combined with the rest of the organisation, they make a useful contribution. It is helpful in this situation to differentiate between the value of the asset (nil) and the value of the business unit which contains the asset (which might be saleable for a large amount).

6.10 There is a well-established technology for valuing business units. In a setting such as this, there are two quite legitimate net realisable values to take into consideration. Skilled experts might easily agree on a nil value for the asset, and also agree on a limited range of positive values for the business unit, while being quite unable to ascribe any computable portion of the latter to the former. Accordingly, we suggest that both numbers are important and should be displayed, the one that does not feature in the main financial statements being noted.

6.11 It will be observed that the historical cost and economic value methods of asset valuation have failed a test each, while replacement cost and net realisable value have passed both, though with some difficulty in each instance.

6.12 In the approach that we are proposing, we advocate the use of net realisable values for the assets of the entity. (The reasons that led us to do so are argued in paragraphs 6.20 – 6.23 below.) We think that there should also be shown the approximate value of the entity's entirety by employing its market capitalisation. We shall discuss these two numbers, and the meaning of any differences between them, as we proceed.

B. MARKET CAPITALISATION

6.13 The value of a company which is quoted on a recognised and liquid stock exchange is most precisely measured during a merger or takeover negotiation, whether hostile or friendly. At that time, the entire business is being sold, by one group of shareholders, to another group. The assets are not (usually) the subject of any separate sale. The sale covers the totality of the entity, which may be worth more or less than the sum of the values of the sub-entities which comprise it. In the case of sales of public companies, it can be assumed that the transaction is entered into by two knowledgeable sets of parties, so that the value arrived at is a fair price.

6.14   The value of the shares of public companies at other times will in general be subject to much less scrutiny. The actively traded alpha stocks are almost certainly kept at a value which is close to the true figure. This assertion does not mean that there will not be combined growth after a merger. A sleepy alpha stock management team may well be truly valued at a low figure; when a livelier management team show signs of taking charge, the existing shareholders will want to share in the resultant gains, but that does not alter the validity of the previous, low, price. (For those not familiar with the expressions, "alpha", "beta" and "gamma" were terms applied at the time of the "Big Bang" to stocks and shares on the basis of the quantities in which they were traded on the exchange. "Alpha" signified those with the largest turnover, "gamma" those with the smallest.)

6.15   Beta and gamma stocks, by definition, receive less attention than alpha stocks. There are fewer traders making the market and fewer shareholders are interested in what they are doing. It is therefore possible that, in the absence of any merger activity, the price at which a beta stock trades may be further away from its "true" value than an alpha would be.

6.16   At the same time, so far as we are aware, there is only one case on record in which the premium on a successful bid for a company quoted on the London exchange was negative. It would seem to follow that the price for which shares are currently quoted on the exchange gives an estimate of the value of the entity which is consistently at or below the true value. The quoted price will be closest to that value during merger negotiations, and below it the rest of the time. The amount by which it is below will be relatively small for alpha stocks, and higher for the less actively traded.

6.17   The market capitalisation, computed by taking the current share price and multiplying by the number of issued shares, is therefore a conservative estimate of the true value of the business. The error is likely to be in the region of 15 – 20% on the average share,

Valuation of Assets and Liabilities

as this has been found to be the average amount of the takeover premium.

6.18 This error is very significantly less than the errors which would be likely to arise if the historical cost book figure were to be used. Such book figures in balance sheets are not intended to have a relationship to market capital values.

6.19 The market value of an entity's shares will be influenced by at least three elements – the market's view of itself as a whole, its view of the industrial class to which the entity belongs and its rating of the entity within that class. While market capitalisation is not a perfect way to arrive at the worth of an entity, it is a measure for which some justification can be made and it is externally verifiable.

C. USE OF NET REALISABLE VALUES

6.20 As explained above, we advocate the use of net realisable value as a relevant basis for helping to appraise an entity's financial wealth. It has much to commend it. Over the years there has been some, though probably minority, academic support for it, and the contributions of Professors Chambers and Sterling have been particularly noteworthy. Its principal merits are:

(a) The values assigned to assets and liabilities may be readily observed in the market place. Where this is the case NRV is as objective as historical costs. We recognise that there may not be a comparable and free market in all the assets and liabilities of an entity but a certain amount of subjectivity will always be present in accounting. Although net realisable values will not under these circumstances be as objective as historical costs, we believe that this will be compensated by increased relevance.

(b) NRV is a value which is readily understandable by investors and other users of accounts. There is evidence to suggest that some external users believe that it is this value which is disclosed by present-day accounts. To make it the actual basis on which assets are valued would go some way towards reducing the "expectation gap" in financial reporting.

(c) Arbitrary decisions about such matters as depreciation are eliminated by the use of NRV because there is no need to allocate the (historical or current) cost of fixed assets to different accounting periods.

(d) The amounts generated by using NRV can be added together

Making Corporate Reports Valuable

and mean something because they are all expressed in current values. This is not true of historical cost accounts in which assets purchased in the latest year are added to those which may have been purchased many years ago. Of course, it is still not true to say that the total of net assets and liabilities given using NRV is indicative of the overall value of an entity. No system of attributing amounts to the identifiable assets and liabilities is. However, this deficiency can be partially overcome by the disclosure of the approximate market capitalisation, as discussed above, which can be compared with the net realisable value of all the identifiable assets and liabilities.

(e) The use of NRV provides information which is likely to be of value to internal and external users of accounts. It is relevant to the evaluation of liquidity in certain instances, which is of considerable importance in appraising the financial position of a company. It is also relevant as a measure of an entity's potential adaptability. The market value of an entity's net assets provides a measure of its ability to change from its present activities to other activities.

(f) The use of NRV would ensure a greater degree of comparability among the financial statements of different entities. Since the assets of all of them would be expressed in terms of current values a comparison of their financial positions would not be distorted by differences in the timing of asset purchases except to the extent that differences in the age of assets affect their current market value.

(g) The use of NRV would also make it easier to appraise individual entities over time because, as indicated in (f) above, the financial position would not be distorted by differences in the timing of asset purchases. The change in the size of the measuring unit which accountants are obliged to use (the £stg in UK) is in the current purchasing power (CPP) of money. For example, any attempt to measure the growth of an entity over a ten year period which does not take into account changes in CPP is likely to mislead, even if it is based on assets and liabilities valued at NRV. For this reason, some restatement in terms of today's CPP is necessary in order to measure "real" growth.

6.21 NRV has merits which make it worthy of consideration as a basis for valuing assets and liabilities. It undoubtedly represents an improvement over present-day accounting and it does appear to be based on commonsense. Some practical issues surrounding

Valuation of Assets and Liabilities

the use of NRV are discussed in paragraphs 6.27 to 6.35.

6.22 The merits of NRV-based accounting systems have been expounded with great conviction and enthusiasm by its proponents over many years but it has not, to date, met with any significant measure of support from professional practising accountants. This has probably been because NRV is also perceived to have some significant disadvantages. The principal arguments against NRV have included:
(a) It has no relevance for a continuing business which has decided not to dispose of its assets but to continue to use them.
(b) For some fixed assets, particularly in the case of specialised, regulated and/or capital intensive industries, it is likely to produce unrealistic values which give no indication of the use value of the assets.
(c) It is likely to produce misleading measures of an entity's performance because under NRV the difference between the worth of a fixed asset at the beginning of a period and its period-end NRV, if lower, is charged as "depreciation" for the period. This decline in worth is unlikely to reflect the use of the asset and may produce meaningless results. For example, in the case of a highly specialised asset with a long expected life but no re-sale value, the purchase price of the asset will be charged as "depreciation" in the year of purchase.

6.23 These are persuasive criticisms in the context of the existing reporting regime but have less force in the context of the new financial disclosures which we suggest in Chapter 7. Taking each of these criticisms in turn:
(a) It is difficult to envisage a business for which liquidity is unimportant, and NRV indicates the potential for liquidity should it be needed. It would also be difficult to justify the decision to continue to use assets without having considered the proceeds which might be received from disposing of them.
(b) The use value of assets which have low NRVs is reflected in the future cash flows which will arise from them. This is an important consideration, and will become apparent if what we suggested in paragraph 6.10 above is adopted as part of the overall package of disclosures that we are suggesting in Chapter 7.
(c) The difficulty of excessive and unrealistic "depreciation" charges is resolved by reflecting the movement between cost and NRV or between opening and closing NRVs through

a Statement of Movement in Financial Wealth and not through the Operations Statement which replaces the traditional profit and loss account. Both these Statements are explained in Chapter 7. The logic behind this reasoning is that it is not necessary to make a charge for the use of fixed assets in measuring operating performance when one is using a value based concept rather than an accruals one. Depreciation charges under the present regime are difficult to calculate with any degree of accuracy being based on a number of subjective estimates. If an asset loses value, the fact will be adequately taken into account in the Statement of Movement in Financial Wealth.

D. REASONS FOR DISREGARDING REPLACEMENT COST

6.24 Whilst current replacement cost accounting has some merits and is an improvement over HC accounting because it evaluates assets in current terms, it has been tried without gaining acceptance and we do not consider it to be as useful as NRV accounting allied to the additional statements and disclosures which we propose. There are particular problems associated with RC accounting, including:
   (a) there is an assumption that assets will be replaced, which is frequently not the case;
   (b) there are significant practical problems in assessing replacement values if there have been improvements in technology; and
   (c) arbitrary depreciation allocations are still required.

6.25 The main reason for not recommending the use of RC as one of the principal bases of asset measurement is that it does not represent worth, being a cost-based measure. Business activity is about the adding of value, so financial statements should reflect this. A value basis rather than a cost basis is therefore predicated. The value of an asset is either the net proceeds which could be realised by selling it or the net present value of the cash flows that can be derived from it. RC is not, in principle, a measure of value.

6.26 There are some circumstances in which RC can be useful, but they are related to *ad hoc* management decisions, not regular reporting of the entity's performance and financial position. For example, replacement cost will be considered among other things when asset replacement decisions have to be made and in

Valuation of Assets and Liabilities

pricing exercises. We agree that RC is appropriate in such circumstances.

E. PRACTICAL CONSIDERATIONS IN USING NET REALISABLE VALUES

6.27 Having satisfied ourselves that there is a case for using NRV as a basis for valuing assets and liabilities, we think it will be helpful to deal with some practical considerations in applying the basis. Our suggestions for that purpose are:
(a) Valuation should be on the basis of orderly disposals unless the circumstances of the entity require that a forced sale be made.
(b) The use of NRV can be applied equally to assets and liabilities although it is recognised that an entity may be less likely to have an option of buying back its liabilities than to find a market for its assets.
(c) Allowance should be made for disposal costs.
(d) As far as practical, individual assets and liabilities should be valued rather than groups of assets.

6.28 Although there is likely to be some scepticism about the use of NRV, it must be admitted that a value can be obtained for most assets if it is required. There are a large number of professional valuers, such as surveyors, architects, auctioneers, insurance assessors and so on who are well-used to valuing assets in circumstances with which accountants may not be familiar.

6.29 The valuation of land and buildings and many other fixed assets is likely to be straightforward. There may not be a ready market for certain specialised items of plant and machinery and so it may not be possible readily to determine their NRV. This does not invalidate the use of the method. If there is *no* market for certain assets, then the economic reality is that their sale value is *nil*. They may well have a use value and we have discussed this earlier.

6.30 There may be a need to make decisions about what to include in an individual asset. For management purposes, it may be desirable for the NRV to be assessed for a subsidiary or a division as a whole so that management can gauge the potential desirability to predators. The idea that subsidiaries or whole divisions could be sold profitably has been a strong factor behind many takeover bids and corporate reorganisations. For external users where consolidated accounts are in question the asset categories of the various group members should be combined. Of course, in the accounts of the holding company itself, investments in subsidiaries will be shown at the net realisable value of the individual entities.

6.31 The valuation of stocks and work-in-progress is also straightforward in principle although we may have to take account of some uncertainties in practice. Accountants and auditors are already thoroughly familiar with the need to calculate NRV in order to apply the "lower of cost or market" rule in historical cost accounting. The rule in NRV accounting simply removes the need to consider cost.

6.32 In many circumstances this method will lead to including unrealised profit in the Operations Statement. Although this may seem like heresy to some accountants, it will be consistent with economic reality provided that realistic estimates of future sales prices and costs to complete are made and the future market for the goods is reasonably assured. In order to be realistic these estimates will have to recognise the possibility of obsolete and/or excess stocks and possible cost-overruns. However, these considerations are nothing new and should cause no insuperable difficulties.

6.33 Receivables and cash and bank balances are already stated at NRV in present-day accounting and will present no new problems.

6.34 The market value of many investments is readily available. In cases where it is not, there are techniques to help estimate values.

6.35 The use of NRV also applies to liabilities. Most liabilities will continue to be stated at the same amounts as at present but in some circumstances adjustments will be required; for example, there is a market in certain long-term corporate debts and market values can change in response to factors such as the general level of interest rates. The market value will be the figure for which the liability can be bought in. In circumstances in which a market value for an entity's liabilities can be determined it should be used in the NRV balance sheet.

SUMMARY

6.36 *In this chapter we have discussed the various bases for applying values to assets and liabilities. We indicated what we believe to be the deficiencies of historical cost and economic value. We noted that current replacement cost and net realisable value both meet our criteria of additivity and reality but we preferred NRV principally because it is value-based whereas RC is cost-based. Value rather than cost is important in assessing financial*

Valuation of Assets and Liabilities

wealth.

6.37 *We also pointed to the importance of knowing the approximate real worth of an entity, the nearest approximation to which is the market capitalisation. Accordingly we discussed this concept and suggested its adoption and comparison with total net identifiable assets at NRV.*

6.38 *Finally we outlined some of the matters to be considered when applying NRV in practice.*

CHAPTER 7

Meeting the Information Needs of Management and Investors

INTRODUCTION

7.1 In preceding chapters we have outlined what we believe management and external users want to know and we have identified shortcomings of contemporary external reporting. We now go on to suggest the kind of package which we believe would be helpful to both parties.

7.2 We see the annual report to investors of both individual entities and groups as coming directly out of management information, though almost certainly not so full, with the only reductions being those that are essential for reasons that are beneficial to the investors. We believe in principle that the latter need the same sort of information as management, both so that the investors are fully informed in the decisions they have to make in relation to their shares, and also so that they are in a position to judge whether the management they have appointed are managing the affairs of the entity properly. It must be borne in mind, however, that some adjustment to the management figures may be necessary to ensure consistency with previous years and/or comparability with other entities.

7.3 In this chapter we take the needs of both management and external users, as identified in Chapter 3, and propose a package of information which, together with the ideas put forward in Chapter 5, we suggest fulfils these needs. We hope that it will become apparent that this package will largely overcome the weaknesses of the present-day reporting system, discussed in Chapter 4.

7.4 Before going into detail, we should like to make clear our belief that, insofar as our suggestions, if adopted, would have a major effect on the corporate report to the investors, we think the changes should be limited initially to quoted companies.

7.5 We have divided up the information requirements of management, which we define as what management require in

Meeting the Information Needs of Management and Investors

order to manage and control the business to the best possible effect, into three main headings, which cover items (a) to (d) of the needs listed in paragraph 3.11 of Chapter 3:
A. Strategy and planning.
B. Information on the present financial status.
C. Information on the probable future financial status.
(Information relating to the environment within which the entity operates is covered in Chapter 5.) Although they should be part of the entire package, we do not in this chapter discuss data on the management of the entity or information about staffing because they should be covered as suggested in Chapter 5. Then there is a further section which gives our views on:
D. The presentation of the information package suggested.
The final section of this chapter refers briefly to the independent assessment of the material published externally.

7.6   Much of the information required under the above headings is available from an entity's internal records but some will have to be obtained externally. We indicate the external material as we come to it.

A. STRATEGY AND PLANNING

7.7   In Chapter 5 we suggested that management needed a statement of the entity's objectives. We also suggested that such a statement should appear in each corporate report.

7.8   In addition, management should have a strategic plan, which will cover several years ahead, a financial plan, which will be for a shorter period, and estimates of future cash flows. These planning documents grow out of each other towards the fulfilment of what have been established as the overall objectives.

7.9   The strategic plan is, we believe, too difficult to "codify" at this stage of development, with very large variations possible, especially in its time scale. Fundamentally, however, it should provide the plan as to how each business sector within the entity will invest, disinvest, market and operate over a certain time scale within the expected economic scenarios to achieve corporate objectives. This plan, unlike the Statement of Objectives, will not normally be made available to external users because of its sensitivity. Knowledge of the overall objectives should provide such users with the ability to judge from the other material in the corporate report what progress is being made towards their achievement.

7.10 The financial plan, which is derived from the strategic plan and will be available to investors in summarised form only, and the estimates of future cash flows are dealt with in more detail later in this chapter.

B. PRESENT FINANCIAL STATUS

7.11 We believe that the ability to judge the wealth of a business at any given time is very necessary for management and would eliminate for external users most of the conceptual problems which afflict present-day accounts and which we discuss in Chapter 4. In Chapter 6 we showed that net realisable value and replacement cost were the best ways of displaying assets in accounts; we also showed that we had chosen NRV because it was a value-based method instead of being cost based and it best met the objective of approximating the financial wealth of a business. The approach to demonstrating financial wealth which we are proposing would involve the preparation of four statements, and we shall discuss them next in this section. These statements are:
(a) Assets and Liabilities Statement;
(b) Operations Statement;
(c) Statement of Changes in Financial Wealth; and
(d) Distributions Statement.

(a) Assets and Liabilities Statement

7.12 The Assets and Liabilities Statement would show the assets and liabilities of the entity at the end of the accounting period, each stated at its net realisable value. Practical considerations about this were discussed in Chapter 6, Section E.

7.13 The normal circumstance will be that the market capitalisation of the entity will be larger than the sum of the net realisable values of the assets shown in the Assets and Liabilities Statement. The difference will be accounted for by the presence in the entity of a host of interacting and complex qualities, such as organisation, corporate culture, staff morale, together with such more obviously measurable (and saleable) items as patents, trademarks, and so on. In addition, there will be variations in the market capitalisation which have nothing to do with the activities of the business. We are not suggesting that it will be possible for each and every one of these items to be identified and assigned a net realisable value. That would be a completely arbitrary exercise at the moment, and we do not think that the

Meeting the Information Needs of Management and Investors

computations will become possible in the foreseeable future. We do, however, recommend it as an area for research. The objective of the Assets and Liabilities Statement is to show the total net realisable assets of the entity, and the market capitalisation, and to highlight the difference. We suggest that the movements in that difference should be subject to useful qualitative comment; it should not be expected that a full quantitative reconciliation will ever be feasible.

7.14 If the entity is in financial trouble, the concept of an orderly disposal of the assets may not be the correct one to apply. In such situations, it will be for the management to decide whether there is a more appropriate method of determining the net realisable values (such as "break-up values"). The independent assessors will also have to apply their minds to the matter.

7.15 The market capitalisation of the entity has already been discussed, and we have stated our belief that it represents the only practical, externally verifiable, estimate of the future cash flows of the business. It is true that most current share quotations represent only a small number of shares, and take account of many external variables in addition. But that is a valid reflection of corporate life in a capitalist environment. It is perfectly possible for an entity to do nothing differently from what it has done in the past, and yet have its market value fall below the net realisable value of its assets because of a sudden change in market sentiment. It is our belief that the annual report should tell the shareholders of public companies about this. If the shareholders conclude that the change is temporary, that is their privilege. If they decide that the change is permanent and that they should sell or that the entity should be wound up, that too is their privilege.

7.16 It may be sensible, however, to average the values of the market capitalisation over a period of a few days before and after the year end. Also, the market capitalisation figure should be labelled clearly, so that investors have every reason to understand that the value for which the entire company could be sold might differ from the calculated market capitalisation.

7.17 We also suggest that a statement should be included which indicates the trend in the share price over the last several weeks before the accounting date. It may be possible to carry this trend report forward to the date upon which the accounts are signed by the directors.

7.18 A simple form of Assets and Liabilities Statement for a holding company might look like this:

Making Corporate Reports Valuable

Market value of property		12,500
Market value of plant		22,170
Market values of subsidiaries		12,984
Market value of other investments		5,468
Market value of vehicles		3,315
Market value of stock and work-in-progress		51,092
Debtors		44,621
Cash		10,471
		162,621
Market value of long loans	(19,231)	
Creditors	(28,008)	
Deferred taxation	(29,304)	
		(76,543)
Net identifiable assets		86,078
Market capitalisation		123,750

Note: There has been a sharp and material increase in the difference between the value of the company as shown by the values of its identifiable individual assets and liabilities, and its market capitalisation as shown by the value of the shares on the London Stock Exchange. The increase is believed to be due to:
(a) The increase in the market for our products, which has made investors regard shares in our sector as growth shares and thus increased the demand.
(b) Rumour of a takeover bid by XYZ plc.
(c) A general rise in the Stock Exchange at a time when the values of our assets less liabilities have risen at a slower rate.
Between the financial year end and the date on which this report was adopted by the Board there was a small rise in the value of our shares (2p per share) on the London Stock Exchange.

7.19 It is assumed that the Assets and Liabilities Statement will be shown for at least one prior period, as is commonplace for balance sheets at present.

7.20 If a business combination were to take place, the assets and liabilities of the two entities would be shown as one after the merger. As these would be aggregated at market value, there would, we suggest, be less room for manipulation than exists in balance sheets at present.

Meeting the Information Needs of Management and Investors

(b) Operations Statement

7.21 The Operations Statement calculates the financial wealth added to the entity by trading and by its operations generally. It differs from the profit and loss account in present use in that:
  (a) there would be no depreciation charge,
  (b) the stock would be accounted for at net realisable value (assuming orderly markets), and
  (c) the only exceptional or extraordinary items would be those arising out of unusual events of a revenue nature; exceptional or extraordinary gains or losses on fixed assets would be dealt with in the Statement of Changes in Financial Wealth outlined below.

7.22 Here is what a simple Operations Statement, which meets the criteria of paragraph 4.9 in Chapter 4, might look like:

Income from continuing activities:		
Sales		307,694
Less Opening stock at market value	(63,535)	
Purchases	(227,677)	
Closing stock at market value	51,092	
	(240,120)	
Operating costs	(31,418)	
		(271,538)
		36,156
Dividend income		920
Income from discontinued operations*		(726)
Income from unusual events*		1,000
Income from prior years not previously accounted for*		(1,716)
		35,634
Less Taxation		(12,760)
Financial wealth added by operations		22,874

* Notes or sub-statements would provide significant details.

(c) Statement of Changes in Financial Wealth

7.23 The Statement of Changes in Financial Wealth which we propose is a statement showing the change in the worth of the business for the period under consideration, such change being split into its main components and indicating how each of these arose.

Making Corporate Reports Valuable

7.24　A simple Statement of Changes in Financial Wealth would look like this:

Financial wealth added by operations		22,874
Increase in value of quoted investment		1,111
Reduction in debenture liability		4,991
		28,976
Decrease in value of plant	(1,089)	
Decrease in value of subsidiary	(3,000)	
Decrease in value of vehicles	(1,466)	
Decrease in value of stock	(3,456)	
		(9,011)
Distributable change in financial wealth for year		19,965
Distribution		(6,444)
		13,521
New share capital		10,000
Change in financial wealth for year		23,521
Movement in market capitalisation		48,750

7.25　The change in financial wealth is measured in terms of year-end pounds. In times of significant inflation it may be helpful if investors can be given an indication of the real change in financial wealth over the period concerned by applying the retail price index to the figure representing the opening net identifiable assets and deducting the result from the change as brought out in the Statement of Changes. This would indicate how the changes in the entity's portfolio of assets related to the change in prices generally.

7.26　If there has been a sale of fixed assets during the period (not assumed in the example above), the Statement of Changes will include the gain or deficiency which will be calculated on the basis of the previous net realisable values.

(d) Distributions Statement

7.27　The fourth statement which we propose would be a Distributions Statement, in which any dividends would be shown. This statement would look like the following:

Meeting the Information Needs of Management and Investors

Distributable change in financial wealth for the year		19,965
Inflation adjustment		–
		19,965
Undistributed surpluses brought forward		21,449
Surpluses available for distribution		41,414
Interim dividend paid	(2,578)	
Final dividend proposed	(3,866)	
		(6,444)
Undistributed surpluses carried forward		34,970

(The foregoing assumes nil inflation for the year.)

7.28 This statement picks up the changes in financial wealth from the statement of that name, together with any retained surpluses from previous periods. While we envisage the dividends being payable out of the increase in the financial wealth of the entity, we recognise that they should be seen in relation to those values which can be realised and also in relation to the cash resources and obligations of the entity.

7.29 It is clearly possible for an entity to wish to make a distribution in a particular year which exceeds the annual total of change in wealth, and which is quite justified in terms of retentions from prior years.

7.30 In times of stable prices, there is no reason why the shareholders should not be permitted to receive any increase in realisable value over the funds they have contributed, whatever the source of that increase. The shareholders should be entitled to share, by means of cash or scrip dividend, in the net increase in financial wealth which has taken place during the year, whether it arises from operations or from changes in the values of assets or liabilities.

7.31 However, during periods of inflation, we feel that the investors should be aware of maintaining the real value of their capital which they supplied at the outset and the effect of any distribution on that real value. To this end we suggest an inflation adjustment, which is shown in the Distributions Statement above, and which might fairly be computed by applying the retail price index to the value of the shareholders' contributed capital as that stood at the start of the year.

7.32 Entities which wish to maintain their operating capability in

Making Corporate Reports Valuable

physical terms could make a further appropriation, if need be, to maintain the asset portfolio or to provide for the replacement of the services which these assets have been supplying.

(e) Examples

7.33 We think the whole concept of the four statements dealt with above may become clearer if we study some examples at this stage. However, so as not to hold up the reading for those who want to go straight on, we have included them at Annex 1 to this chapter. They deal with two situations which are not unusual but which illustrate the way in which the suggested presentation brings out salient features not ascertainable from the normal profit and loss account and balance sheet. The figures which we have used are not intended to be significant, only to illustrate the effect of the statements.

7.34 The foregoing statements are the means by which the management and the external users can see the state of an entity's financial wealth at a given time and how it has changed since the previous report. However, they do not provide all the information needed to understand the changes that have taken place during the period. We now go on to discuss what is needed in addition to the four basic statements already described.

(f) Cash Flow Statement

7.35 We regard this as essential for any board of directors and for investors. It is something which not all boards see at the moment, and it is not a statement which investors ever see, though the existing source and application of funds statement, which is different in concept, goes some way towards meeting this need. We think much more emphasis requires to be given to this aspect of business management.

7.36 We define the statement as one showing the inflow and outflow of cash broken down into its main components, and usually dealing with the year of the accounts and going three years forward. The figures will normally be shown by months, but for external reporting we suggest that they cover a year, with significant peaks and troughs highlighted and compared with overdraft and other facilities available.

7.37 It is interesting to note that a recent statement by the Financial Accounting Standards Board (FASB) in the USA requires a statement of cash flows as part of a full set of financial statements of all business entities. This statement of cash flows will classify cash receipts and payments by operating, investing and financing cash flows. The FASB is making the statement effective for financial periods ending after 15 July 1988. Such cash flows will be only historical.

7.38 An example of a cash flow statement for external users follows:

Opening Balance	(6,016)
Generated by Operations	18,320
Investments:	
Fixed assets	(16,500)
Quoted shares (trade investment)	(3,333)
New Finance:	
Debentures	8,000
Share capital	10,000
Closing Balance	10,471

(g) Necessary Segments

7.39 We believe that all the statements mentioned above will be inadequate for both managements' and external users' purposes if there is just the one statement for the whole entity. We think they will all need to be split in various ways, as discussed in Chapter 5, and particularly we feel that, provided the amounts are significant, there should be a split:
(i) By product.
(ii) By manufacturing location.
(iii) Geographically.
(iv) By currency.
However, the actual divisions will depend very much on the size and complexity of the entity involved.

7.40 Just to take one example, the geographic split might be by towns, by counties, by countries or even by continents. We think it is impossible to be dogmatic about the type of geographic split required. There may also be particular reasons, for example from the point of view of competition or for political reasons in a country, why some of this information should not be given in public documents, eg to investors. We see it as being part of the role of the new form of audit (the independent assessment) to ensure that as far as the investors are concerned they are given a sensible division for the four categories mentioned above, subject to this not creating serious problems which could affect the health of the business and therefore be to their own detriment.

Making Corporate Reports Valuable

7.41 Regarding the level of detail, there is no doubt that the systems in use in managing the company would produce far more detail than investors, employees and creditors would want. The level of detail that makes sense for a big corporation (which will normally entail several hierarchical levels of reporting detail) will not usually make sense for smaller enterprises. The amount of detail which should be made available must also depend on the reportee's ability to digest information rather than on the ability of accountants to sub-divide information on an entity into components of various kinds.

7.42 It is likely, however, that certain user groups will want to receive more information than others. It is possible, making use of modern technology, to provide these users with such information. The full detailed figures, broken down as far as can be justified by confidentiality, could be placed in a general access file in an entity's computer and updated as often as required. Those users who need the detail could be provided with a phone number which would link their computer directly to this file, which they could copy on to their own machine and carry out computations as desired. The objective would be to use the information base to enhance the relationship of an entity to the finance markets by making it easier for users to access the data they want. (ICI have made major inroads in the paint and agricultural markets by providing very similar kinds of access to their product selection computers.)

(h) Other necessary information

7.43 Included in the package of information for management and in the one for investors would be the statements which we suggest in Chapter 5 could be introduced in a reasonably short space of time and which are not given externally at present.

7.44 To save looking back, the following is a list of the statements and additional disclosures that we have in mind:
For both directors and external users:
(a) information on related parties (5.16);
(b) information on accounting areas subject to uncertainty (5.17);
(c) statement on relative innovation (5.18);
(d) information on effectiveness and lead-time of research and development (5.19);
(e) information on the economic environment (5.41 – 5.43);
(f) comparative operational statistics (5.44); and
(g) information on staff resources (5.47 – 5.50).

Meeting the Information Needs of Management and Investors

For external users only:
(h) information on ownership, management and their responsibilities (5.35, 5.45, 5.46).

C. FUTURE FINANCIAL STATUS

7.45 We touched in Chapter 5 upon the need for external users to have future-orientated information. We now pursue this idea further, commencing with a review of the normal financial planning practices which managements undertake, before considering what the investors should be provided with.

(a) Financial Plans

7.46 We believe that boards should have, in most cases, a three year financial plan, probably split year by year and possibly in the shorter term into shorter periods of time. It differs from the cash flow statement by dealing with value and not cash. It will therefore embrace figures in the estimated future Operations Statements and movements in the value of the assets and liabilities shown in the Assets and Liabilities Statement. It would not, however, be expected to bring in market capitalisation figures because we do not believe it is realistic to expect management to estimate the market value of their own shares for such a future period.

7.47 The three year period has been chosen because we understand that most businesses find this the optimum period for such plans, but the term should be that most appropriate to the business concerned. The financial plan should not be "cast in stone" but should be subject to regular revision, and we believe that consideration of the need for change in the financial plan, often arising because the original assumptions have proved to be incorrect, is probably of more value to most boards of directors than the current comparison of "actual to budget", which tends to be dealing with history rather than with the future and the planning that has to come from it. The financial plan will need in many cases to be adjustable for sensitivity factors (for example, what is the effect on the plan if parity rates for currency, instead of being as forecast, were to be, say, 10% higher or lower).

7.48 While as stated above we believe that the reasons for changes in the financial plan need more discussion than the actual out-turn compared to the latest financial plan, the comparison of "actual to budget" should not be omitted, but should be regarded as having

Making Corporate Reports Valuable

reduced importance. This comparison of actual to budget would therefore still be used for control purposes, but not for planning purposes.

7.49 Within the financial plan (and also within the cash flow) would be the major projects for expansion or investment and their outturn.

7.50 A summary of the financial plan should be provided to the investors. This summary should be based upon the current methods used in preparing a prospectus, which normally (depending on the exact date of the proposed share issue) will include a forecast financial report for the coming year. It could, however, be longer if management so decided. Also, we suggest that the major assumptions which have been used by management in preparing the three year financial plan should be disclosed, even though the plan itself is for a shorter period. These major assumptions would be of the type that are fundamental to future-orientated material that has to be published in prospectus or takeover documents today: they would not be required to cover every detail of management's forward thinking.

7.51 Management should provide a discussion of the differences between the financial plan disclosed in last year's report and the actual results for the year. This discussion would enable the investor to:
 (a) see the view of the future held by management then and now;
 (b) appraise management's ability to forecast;
 (c) consider the problems which may have afflicted the entity during the year under review; and
 (d) estimate the likely trend of future dividends.

(b) Future Cash Flows

7.52 As well as the statement of cash flows for the current year it will be necessary for the management to have a forecast of the cash flows to come. In paragraph 7.36 three years forward were suggested. These projections should also be available to external users in summarised form, for at least one year forward (but longer if management thought it desirable).

Summary

7.53 We see the information relating to the future which will be before management and investors as comprising:

Meeting the Information Needs of Management and Investors

(a) narrative statement of the entity's objectives (supported for management by a strategic plan);
(b) forward financial plan (probably three years for management, at least one year for external users); and
(c) statement of future cash flows covering the same periods.

D. PRESENTATION OF INFORMATION

(a) Layering

7.54 For both management and external users the way in which information about an entity is presented and the interval of time between the event and its reporting are extremely important. Management will, of course, arrange that their reports are in whatever form they find most suitable, but we suggest that the principle of "layering" can be very helpful. It means that each statement starts with the simplest possible presentation of the main factors and, as the reader works through the information available, it can be called down in layers of increasing complexity and detail. The purpose of this is so that management, and particularly the board of directors, can go down to the level of detail they desire, which may vary from individual to individual and between executive and non-executive directors. Equally, the directors can then decide the cut-off layer of information above which it is presented to the investors. Using this method for external reporting would eliminate the copious notes with which readers are currently faced because the detail which such notes would contain could be made available in one of the lower layers.

(b) Timeliness

7.55 Management can normally call for information whenever they want it but for external users reporting annually may seem rather anachronistic. The rate of change these days is too fast, it may be thought, for this method to inform the interested groups rapidly enough. Taking this together with the developments in information technology, it would seem perfectly feasible for a full corporate report to be produced as a sub-set of the reports which are prepared for senior management as often as those reports are provided. Furthermore, it would be feasible for this information to be put on one of the electronic distribution networks at very small cost to the company.

7.56 Drawbacks foreseen in implementing this frequent availability of

Making Corporate Reports Valuable

information *via* computer include:

(i) the danger of giving away too much information too soon so that the entity concerned would be unable to take advantage of business opportunities;

(ii) entities would wish to continue to choose the moment to go public on certain issues (an example of this might be closure of a factory. As soon as a decision was made it would presumably have to be accounted for in the periodical reports, whereas the entity might prefer to delay the announcement until nearer the actual closure date); and

(iii) the danger of giving too much data but not enough information (the scenario is envisaged of a computer dialling up other computers, finding out the sales figure was down on budget and then the computer as programmed would start selling the shares – the message is that information should be distributed at human pace).

7.57 Arising out of the discussion in the two preceding paragraphs, we think that corporate reports should continue to be prepared annually but that during the year quoted companies (and also in due course major unquoted ones) should be required to report results by three-monthly periods and significant "events" as they occur. By events reporting we would be seeking to formalise to a large extent what is present practice and to ensure that information is available publicly as soon as possible in an effort to eliminate insider dealing. Companies should be required to disclose "events" sufficiently important to affect anyone's view of an entity within three days of the happening of the event, subject inevitably to exceptions that would be seriously prejudicial to the business if disclosed at that point of time. (Perhaps The Stock Exchange or the independent assessors might be required to consider in retrospect whether a delay of an announcement was justified.) This would include announcements on confirmed contracts, litigations, acquisitions or disposals, significant variances from the annual forecast, etc.

7.58 The foregoing reporting procedures would largely be carried out by means of the computer. There would however continue to be a need to produce information in hard copy for investors and other user groups who might not have, or want to have, access to information available *via* computer.

E. INDEPENDENT ASSESSMENT

7.59 We are in no doubt that an independent assessment will require to be made of the new information which we believe should appear in external corporate reports. Readers of the reports will need some sort of assurance that the information is not just a figment of somebody's imagination. Equally we are in no doubt that the independent assessor cannot be expected to provide the same sort of assurance about "soft" information (that is, certain estimates, assumptions and future-orientated material) as the auditor does now for the harder information contained in historical cost financial statements.

7.60 We do not foresee any particular technical difficulties for the assessor in forming a view about assumptions made by management in relation to future plans and other forward projections, or about non-quantitative information. External assistance may be required in making judgments on the realisable values of some assets, but this is nothing new. Auditors have never been valuers and have had to seek help with assets of a special nature.

7.61 We think that tomorrow's independent assessment teams will have to include disciplines other than accounting. There is already a trend in this direction, and the profession will require to give thought to the implications for discipline, training and quality control.

7.62 As information becomes publicly available *via* computer terminals, it seems likely that the independent assessor will have to have continuous procedures for monitoring the data bases. These procedures should produce to the assessor whatever exception reports may be necessary. He will also have to be almost continuously considering those areas of judgment inherent in any package of financial information. Instead of dealing with such matters once a year, at each annual financial statement date, he could well have to consider them on a monthly basis or even more frequently. Any call for the assessment of information on a quarterly basis, for example, could be met by this procedure.

7.63 An important advantage of this continuous monitoring would be the independent assessor becoming aware at a very early stage of any critical breakdown in the system for providing the necessary

Making Corporate Reports Valuable

information. We believe that if this happens the assessor should have a legal right to report the situation to some external regulator (eg the Department of Trade and Industry), which would be responsible for deciding what action should be taken (inform the shareholders, appoint inspectors, make the matter public or whatever).

7.64 The independent assessor's report on the new information package will need to be long-form. We think it should be specific to the circumstances of the particular client and, therefore, *ad hoc*. It will be more interesting and more readable than contemporary audit reports and achieve the basic purpose of communicating further and useful information to the reader. Such a report, after all, will be an integral part of the corporate report envisaged and will be seeking to communicate just as effectively as the other information contained in the corporate report. A suggestion of the sort of information that might be given in a long-form report by an independent assessor is given in Annex 2 to this chapter.

7.65 We think that, in addition to the independent assessor presenting his own report in clear and understandable terms, he should also make an assessment of whether the information included in the financial statements is presented in such a way that it will be comprehensible to a reasonable person. If he has any doubts, we suggest that he tries to dispel the obfuscation in his own report.

7.66 In summary we believe that tomorrow's independent assessor can meet, and be part of, the innovations suggested in this and earlier chapters. He will have different skills and a far wider scope to his work, with the much greater emphasis in the corporate report on market values and future plans. This will place demands on him which today's auditor does not have to meet (except, perhaps, in prospectus-type work) and will require implicit judgment of much that management is doing or plans to do.

7.67 The skills and expertise that the assessor will need will place considerable pressure on education and training in order to equip him for this future; other disciplines will also be part of the assessment team. The team, however, will still be operating in a function substantially based on the procurement and evaluation of evidence.

7.68 The overall effect should be a report which is more interesting and meaningful to its recipients and more satisfying to all concerned.

Meeting the Information Needs of Management and Investors

SUMMARY

7.69 *In this chapter we proposed an entirely new information package which can be used for both management and external purposes. We explained that the only difference between the two packages would be a reduced amount of information to external users in circumstances where the reduction would be beneficial to investors. We also suggested that initially the package should apply to quoted companies only.*

7.70 *We developed our views on strategic and planning documents – the Statement of Objectives, the Strategic Plan, the Financial Plan and the Estimate of Future Cash Flows.*

7.71 *With a view to disclosing the financial wealth of an entity and the changes in it, we suggested four basic statements – the Assets and Liabilities Statement, the Operations Statement, the Statement of Changes in Financial Wealth and the Distributions Statement. These are explained and illustrated. We also suggested additional information necessary to a proper understanding of an entity's current position.*

7.72 *We suggested "layering" the information package for both internal and external users so that individuals could reach the level of detail suitable for them. We also discussed the use of electronic means to convey the information to external users, and concluded that there should be annual, independently assessed reports, three-monthly reports of results and reports of significant events as they occur.*

7.73 *We stated our belief in the need for independent assessment of the information published externally and in the ability of independent assessors to undertake the necessary procurement and evaluation of evidence. We foresaw, however, the use of multi-disciplinary assessment teams and continuous monitoring of data. We favoured a long-form,* ad hoc *type of report for each entity.*

ANNEX 1

Examples of the way in which the four basic statements bring out relevant information

Example 1
Let us start with a very simple example, a one ship company, with

Making Corporate Reports Valuable

a five year charter to a reputable counterparty, signed within the year, the ship having been financed by a "soft" (ie at below market rates of interest) loan. We assume that prices have remained stable during the year.

Today the accounts would show, ignoring tax:

Balance Sheet

Share Capital	22,500	Ship at Cost	80,000
Balance of P&L		Less	
A/C	9,500	depreciation	(28,000)
Creditors	3,000		
Loan	20,000	Cash	3,000
	55,000		55,000

Profit and Loss Account

Income from Charter	8,600
Interest	(1,600)
Depreciation	(4,000)
Net Profit	3,000

These statements make it difficult to assess objectives, performance etc. However, under our proposals the increase in wealth, the way in which it has come about (the wealth added by operations and from other sources) and the amount of the increase distributable to shareholders become clear.

The new statements would show:

Assets and Liabilities Statement

Market Value of Ship	20,000
Market Value of Charter	35,000
Cash	3,000
	58,000
Less Creditors	(3000)
Market Value of Soft Loan	(16,000)
Net identifiable assets	39,000
Market Capitalisation	54,000

Meeting the Information Needs of Management and Investors

Operations Statement

Income from charter	8,600
Less Interest	(1,600)
Wealth added by operations	7,000

Statement of Changes in Financial Wealth

Wealth added by operations	7,000
Increase in value through having signed charter	35,000
Change in value of soft loan through rise in interest rates	4,000
	46,000
Decrease in market value of ship	(36,000)
Distributable change in financial wealth for the year	10,000
Distribution	(5,000)
Change in financial wealth for year	5,000
Change in market capitalisation	24,000

Distributions Statement

Distributable change in financial wealth for the year		10,000
Undistributed surpluses brought forward		6,500
Surpluses available for distribution		16,500
Interim dividend paid	(2,000)	
Final dividend proposed	(3,000)	
		(5,000)
Undistributed surpluses carried forward		11,500

Example 2

For the second example, we take an old distillery in the Highlands of Scotland, with old buildings and machinery which, with the current overproduction of Scotch, no-one would buy, but with a good stream of clear water and still producing and selling a good malt whisky.

Making Corporate Reports Valuable

Under present conditions, the accounts would show:

Balance Sheet

Share Capital	27,000	Buildings at cost	
Balance of P&L A/C	8,500	Less deprec'n	15,000
Creditors	10,500	Machinery at cost	
		Less deprec'n	9,000
		Stock at cost	16,500
		Debtors	4,500
		Cash	1,000
	46,000		46,000

Profit and Loss Account

Sales	30,000
Cost of sales	(14,500)
Operating costs	(9,000)
Depreciation	(5,000)
Profit for Year	1,500

Under the suggested system, what would show would be:

Assets and Liabilities Statement

Market Value of Buildings	NIL
Market Value of Machinery	NIL
Market Value of Stock	22,000
Debtors	4,500
Cash	1,000
	27,500
Less Creditors	(10,500)
Net identifiable assets	17,000
Market capitalisation	40,000

Note: The market capitalisation exceeds the net identifiable assets by £23,000 compared with £5,000 last year. The stock market has risen by 10% during the year, but our industrial sector has remained steady. Apart from external factors affecting the stock market, the amount of £18,000 is principally accounted for by the value of future cash flows, which we have not attempted to quantify, arising from goodwill in the name of the malt whisky, the value of

Meeting the Information Needs of Management and Investors

the marketing staff who make the sales possible, the value of the advertising, the value of the staff who operate the machinery making the whisky, etc. This has been offset by the writing down of the values of buildings and machinery, which, in practical terms, have no realisable value.

Operations Statement

Income from continuing operations:

Sales	30,000
Cost of sales	(9,000)
Operating costs	(9,000)
Wealth added by operations	12,000

Statement of Change in Financial Wealth

Wealth added by operations	12,000
Decrease in market value of buildings	(16,000)
Decrease in market value of machinery	(13,000)
Decrease in financial wealth for year	(17,000)
Change in market capitalisation	1,000

The Distributions Statement will be similar to the previous example except that the change in financial wealth for the year will be negative.

ANNEX 2

Suggested outline of the contents of an independent assessor's long-form report

The basic elements of the report should include the following:

Financial Statements

(a) a statement that the financial statements were subjected to independent assessment;
(b) a statement that the financial statements are the representations of management (including the management's judgment of any future events likely to affect the current position);

(c) a statement that the assessment was performed in accordance with the standards laid down by the recognised accountancy bodies;
(d) a statement that the assessment process was designed to enable a view to be taken on whether the financial statements are materially misstated (intentionally or unintentionally);
(e) a discussion of the factors involved in achieving reasonable assurance as a result of that assessment:
   (i) by examining, on a test basis, evidence that supports the amounts included in the financial statements;
   (ii) by assessing the appropriateness of the accounting policies used and the estimates made by management; and
   (iii) by assessing the appropriateness of the overall financial statement presentation and disclosures;
(f) a statement that the independent assessor believes that the procedures performed were appropriate in the circumstances to express the opinion presented;
(g) a statement of the independent assessor's opinion of the view shown by the financial statements; and
(h) confirmation that the law relating to financial reporting has been complied with.

Internal Controls and Accounting Records

(a) a statement that management are responsible for establishing and maintaining adequate accounting records and internal control systems;
(b) a statement that the objective of the control system is to provide reasonable but not absolute assurance that assets are safeguarded against loss from unauthorised use or theft and that the business can be controlled on the basis of useful information. In fulfilling their responsibility management must formulate a view on whether the expected benefits of the control systems outweigh the costs of the control systems themselves;
(c) a warning that because of inherent limitations in any internal control system errors or thefts may nevertheless occur and not be detected; and
(d) a statement that, in addition, the projection of any assessment of the system to future periods is subject to the risk that the procedures may become inadequate because of changes in conditions or that the degree of compliance with

Meeting the Information Needs of Management and Investors

the procedures may deteriorate.

Future Information

(a) an expression of opinion as to whether:
   (i) the assumptions, which are the sole responsibility of management, provide a reasonable basis for the preparation of the forecasts; and
   (ii) the forecast has been appropriately prepared on the basis of the assumptions;
(b) a warning that the actual results are likely to be different from the forecast since anticipated events frequently do not occur as expected and the variation could, in certain cases, be material; and
(c) a statement that if the plans are fulfilled they would meet the entity's agreed objectives.

General

(a) a statement that the assessor agreed with the board in the non-disclosure of certain information, the publication of which could lead to competitive disadvantage; and
(b) a note of any aspect of the financial statements which the independent assessor believes should be specially drawn to readers' attention.

CHAPTER 8

Conclusions

A. THE CASE FOR CHANGE

8.1 One of our beliefs when we began this study was that the efficient working of a securities market requires effective communication of information by managements to investors. Studies undertaken seem to indicate that there is inadequate communication between the two parties, to the improvement of which present-day corporate reports do not appear to make a worthwhile contribution.

8.2 In Chapter 4 we summarised a number of aspects of contemporary accounting and reporting which leave something to be desired. We drew attention to the fact that the financial statements are in a form very difficult to understand, that they are based on no consistent conceptual validity and that they do not in many cases represent economic reality.

8.3 Other criticisms of the present regime include the time-lag between the date when events take place and the time when the statements recording them are published, the claim (at any rate by sophisticated users) that insufficient useful information is given (for example, on segments and on the future) and that the audit report, particularly if qualified, is not easy to understand.

8.4 Given findings of this kind, we concluded that our belief, that present-day corporate reports based on the historical cost convention are not satisfactory, was justified and we sought ideas as to how they could be improved. In Chapter 5 we put forward some shorter-term suggestions and in Chapter 7 we outlined a complete new reporting package which we believe would go a long way towards informing more effectively the external users of reports about their entity's wealth and progress.

B. THE BENEFITS

8.5 Some of the benefits which we would expect of our new package – though, as we have indicated, they would probably not be felt fully until some ten to fifteen years hence – are now considered for each of the potential beneficiaries.

Conclusions

(a) Managements

8.6 We believe the form in which we suggest information be presented will be an improvement on some forms at present in use. We hope, therefore, that it will help some directors and senior managers to understand more clearly than before many of the matters which they are called upon to consider.

8.7 Where internal reporting is below a good standard – as unfortunately is the case in some entities – our suggestions could point the way to improving the standard.

8.8 If, as we believe, most managements are keen that The Stock Exchange quotation of their entities should be at least maintained, the greater external disclosure should help to improve the efficiency of the market and therefore the accuracy of the entity's standing in the market.

8.9 Managements will be taking their shareholders more into their confidence and this must surely improve the relationship between the two parties.

(b) External users

8.10 Better communication and increased information should enable external users to monitor the activities of management better, and to take action more quickly if something appears to be going wrong and management do not appear to be doing something about it.

8.11 So far as investors are concerned, the market should have more and better information to assist in the setting of share prices, and the scope for insider activity should be curtailed. This ought to lead to a fairer market for the ordinary investor.

8.12 Investors will also become better informed, which will help them in making their investment decisions, and their responsibilities to determine or influence policy will become more explicit.

(c) The country as a whole

8.13 Sleepy managements should become more apparent, which ought to lead to their becoming more awake or to their being replaced by more active individuals. In either case, the efficiency of business generally within the country should improve.

8.14 This in turn should lead to a better allocation of resources within entities and among entities, with a consequent improvement in the financial state of those entities and of those who invest in them. This should benefit the economy as a whole.

Making Corporate Reports Valuable

8.15 It is to be hoped that the type of information given and the manner of its presentation will commend themselves to government departments concerned and will so reduce the amount of additional information that has to be sought.

(d) Company accountants

8.16 These are the people within entities who have to prepare the internal and external reports. Because they will be using the information prepared for management they will be relieved of the hassle caused by the periodical external report other than removing sensitive items and summarising in certain instances. This should enable them to devote their attention to more profitable activities.

C. THE IMPLICATIONS

8.17 Before a corporate report package along the lines suggested in Chapter 7 could be introduced in any country there would be much that would have to be done. In the following paragraphs we outline what we see as the implications for various sectors of society.

(a) Managements

8.18 Clearly managements will want to study our suggestions and consider how they would affect internal and external reporting within their own entities. It is our hope that many of them would like to experiment with both the shorter- and the longer-term ideas (bearing in mind that they could be introduced into existing reports as supplementary information).

8.19 Both international and domestic managements will also wish to consider the implications of the laws, regulations, standards and conventions which apply in the various countries where they operate.

8.20 They will obviously have to consider the costs of implementing our suggestions and form an opinion on whether the expected benefits to themselves and to those to whom they report (which are probably unquantifiable) justify their adopting them.

Conclusions

(b) External users

8.21 We should like to think that all classes of external users (and especially analysts acting on behalf of investors and loan creditors) will study the suggestions and form a view as to the additional help which will be provided by them. When satisfied about the benefits, they might wish to make representations that the changes which we have suggested be introduced.

8.22 Some loan creditors and some employees have contracts with entities which are tied to figures in the financial statements drawn up under the existing regime (eg the limitation of borrowings on the basis of historical cost balance sheets and executive remuneration based on results shown by historical cost profit and loss accounts). Such contracts will need reconsideration and, it is to be hoped, adjustment to the revised regime. In the meantime, however, it will probably be necessary to continue maintaining figures on an historical cost basis. This would allow for the calculations under the terms of existing contracts; it would also facilitate taxation computations while the present tax system continues to operate.

(c) Governments

8.23 Much of what is given in present-day corporate reports is there because the law requires it. Relevant government departments would need to review the law to see what changes would be required if our package were to be adopted in lieu of the present one. They too, will wish to satisfy themselves of the benefits to be obtained from a new regime.

8.24 In the United Kingdom company law covering the format and content of financial statements, the appointment and duties of auditors, distributions, business combinations and so on will call for review and, if need be, amendment. To achieve that would involve the European Commission and other countries within the European Community.

(d) Securities authorities

8.25 These, like government, will obviously want to review the suggestions and form views on their benefits. They will also want to consider them in the light of any regulations they have issued and of what amendments they might entail.

(e) Professional accountancy bodies

8.26 These will require to consider the implications for all their members, for the public whom those members serve and for themselves. It is to be hoped that they will be sufficiently persuaded of the merits of our case to institute research projects into those aspects which still require elaboration, and also into the costs and benefits of adopting our suggestions.

8.27 They will particularly need to think about education and training for the future, independence, disciplinary procedures and other aspects of their professional sphere of influence in the light of multi-disciplinary auditing firms and virtually on-line financial reporting.

8.28 Accounting and auditing standards and guidelines will certainly require reconsideration and we would hope that our suggestions would lead to a reduction in the number of mandatory pronouncements (what is sometimes referred to as "the standards overload").

(f) Auditors

8.29 There are many implications in what we suggest for the auditors of the future (the independent assessors). The scope of their work will be widened and they will wish to evaluate how the additional matters can best be handled. They will also wish to consider (and probably advise government) about the terms in which they can report. Our suggestions in Annex 2 to Chapter 7 could provide a starting point for debate.

8.30 They will also need to consider what implications (if any) their additional responsibilities might have on their potential liability to litigation. If need be, they might make appropriate submissions to government for alleviating any extra burden, since it would hardly benefit anyone if the auditing profession were driven to abandon its responsibilities because of a constant fear of being sued.

(g) Researchers

8.31 We have tried to provide a coherent focus for future research effort. We hope that researchers, particularly in academe, will study our suggestions and adopt some of them for deeper investigation, especially as the outcome could make a valuable contribution to practice. We should very much like to see a project which would produce a corporate report on the basis of

Conclusions

our suggestions and compare it with one under current conditions. In Chapter 9 we have summarised those other issues which we think especially call for further research.

SUMMARY

8.32 *In this chapter we have summarised what persuaded us to suggest a new information package for both internal and external users. We have outlined some of the benefits which we hope the adoption of such a package would have for various interested parties. Finally we have indicated what the implications of our suggestions are likely to be for managements, external users, governments, securities authorities, professional accountancy bodies, auditors and researchers.*

CHAPTER 9

Summary of Our Suggestions

BASIC CONCLUSIONS

9.1 In Chapter 1 we reviewed the considerations that had led us to undertake this study. The basic conclusions to which we came were recorded in that Chapter, namely that since we believe an efficient market requires the communication of useful information from managements to investors (1.8):
   (a) financial reports ought to portray economic reality (1.2); and
   (b) the information needed by investors is the same in kind, but not in volume, as that needed by managements (1.12, 3.3, 7.2).

9.2 Also in that Chapter, and in more detail in Chapter 4, we suggested reasons why present-day corporate reports are not satisfactory. They concentrate too much on the legal form of transactions rather than their economic substance, they concentrate on the past to the exclusion of the future, they concentrate on cost rather than value and they pay too much attention to "profit" and not enough to wealth (1.13).

9.3 We followed this latter thought up in Chapter 5, where we suggested that the total wealth of an entity and the changes in it should be of major importance to both managements and investors (5.3). We returned to it in Chapter 7 (7.11) and proceeded to show in the subsequent paragraphs of that chapter how such information might be presented.

9.4 As regards basing financial statements on value, we expressed a preference for the use of net realisable values (5.7, 6.1, 7.11). We outlined our reasons for that preference in paragraphs 6.20–6.23 inclusive of Chapter 6.

USERS OF CORPORATE REPORTS

9.5 We discussed those to whom there should be communication by way of corporate reports in Chapter 3. We suggested that these were:
   (a) the equity investor group;
   (b) the loan creditor group;

Summary of Our Suggestions

(c) the employee group; and
(d) the business contact group (3.6).
We explained why we had not included the analyst-adviser group (3.9), the government and the general public (3.10) in our list.

9.6 We accepted that the potential needs of all users were unlikely to be met by general purpose reports (3.7).

9.7 We suggested that users ought not to be faced with reports that have to be "translated" for them (3.8), a point to which we returned in Chapter 5 (5.32).

9.8 We suggested that managements should not give information to analysts which they do not give to other external users at the same time (3.9).

9.9 We outlined what we thought to be the fundamental information needs of external users:
   (a) information on an entity's objectives and its performance towards achieving them;
   (b) a comparison of an entity's total wealth now as against that at the previous reporting date, and the reasons for the change;
   (c) the entity's likely future status, performance and resources;
   (d) the present and projected environment of the entity; and
   (e) information on the ownership and control of the entity and on the background of its management (3.11 – 3.13).

9.10 We noted that some creditors and employees may, for the time being, need accounts drawn up under the existing regime. (But we hoped this need would be short-term.) (8.22)

INFORMATION FOR MANAGEMENTS

9.11 In this study we considered the information needs of both managements and external users. The bulk of our suggestions for a management package are in Chapter 7, which we deal with below (9.47 – 9.55) under the title of "Long-term improvements in reporting internally and externally". Our other suggestions, which come forward in earlier chapters, are given below.

9.12 We expressed a view that information coming before boards of directors ought to be as comprehensive as possible, and that the present published accounts are normally irrelevant for making fundamental decisions (3.2). In elaboration of the last-mentioned point, we referred to the need to consider the future more than the past, for which published accounts are almost never used (5.38).

9.13 We pointed out that not all directors and managers are equally

Making Corporate Reports Valuable

numerate and that for many it is helpful to present financial information in descriptive form (3.4).

9.14 We suggested that managements' fundamental information needs are covered by points (a) to (d) inclusive in paragraph 9.9 above (3.14).

9.15 A Statement of Corporate Objectives, reviewed by the directors on a regular basis, seemed to us necessary for management (5.4). We explained the supporting documents to that Statement in paragraphs 7.8 – 7.10 inclusive of Chapter 7.

9.16 We saw a need for managements to have a plan to meet short- and long-term staff requirements (5.48).

EXTERNAL REPORTING

9.17 As we believed that external users need to be able to form a view about an entity's future (3.11(c)), it seemed to us that the future-orientated information which managements use should, up to a point, be available to investors (5.38).

9.18 We suggested some benefits of wider external disclosure:
   (a) less likelihood of insiders taking unfair advantage;
   (b) enhancement of the efficiency of the market for securities;
   (c) better control of investors over managements;
   (d) firmer base for investors' judgments; and
   (e) enhancement of the reputations of forward-looking entities (3.19).

9.19 We did, however, sound a warning note on extended external reporting, namely that to give some information could be detrimental to the investors (3.20). We repeated this point in relation to segmental reporting (7.40).

9.20 We thought that technical jargon should be avoided in external reports as far as possible; if there is no alternative, the technical term should be defined (5.33).

9.21 Our suggestions for detailed improvements in corporate reporting should initially be limited to quoted companies (7.4).

9.22 Our view that the timeliness of corporate reports could be improved by electronic distribution methods (7.55) did not alter our opinion that such reports should be prepared annually (7.57). We did think, however, that there should be three-monthly interim reports and the reporting of "events" as they occur (7.57).

9.23 In addition to the foregoing general points, we suggested in Chapter 5 a number of solutions for the unsatisfactory nature of

Summary of Our Suggestions

present financial statements. These, we thought, could be adopted within a reasonably short space of time, and we summarise them in the following paragraphs of this section.

9.24 Every corporate report should contain a Statement of Objectives or a summary of it (5.5).

9.25 The emphasis on prudence required under existing UK company law should be dropped (5.10).

9.26 There should be a statement showing all the changes in an entity's financial wealth (5.12).

9.27 Additional segmental information should be given (5.13 – 5.14). This was referred to also in connection with market information (5.43).

9.28 Related parties should be identified and significant transactions with them disclosed (5.16).

9.29 Information should be given on:
   (a) areas of accounting subject to uncertainty and the boundaries of uncertainty;
   (b) significant estimated amounts and possible margins of error; and
   (c) expenditure, the timing of which can be discretionary (5.17).

9.30 There should be a Statement of Relative Innovation (5.18).

9.31 The effectiveness and lead time of significant research and development should be disclosed (5.19).

9.32 It would be helpful to disclose the market capitalisation figure and to have a comment on the difference between it and the published financial wealth (5.21). The subject of market capitalisation is pursued further in paragraphs 6.13 – 6.19 inclusive of Chapter 6.

9.33 Because we did not believe that merger accounting provides a true and fair view (4.15), we suggest the fullest disclosure of what has been done when that method is used and a comparison of what the result would have been using the acquisition method (5.22).

9.34 There should be disclosure of results for the whole of the combination year and of what part of the results of a combined business relate to the pre-combination period (5.23).

9.35 In business combination cases reorganisation provisions should be written off as an unusual item in the year of combination (5.24).

9.36 The nature of goodwill should always be carefully explained (5.25).

9.37 The treatment in consolidated accounts of associated companies

Making Corporate Reports Valuable

should depend upon the degree of influence, and managements should obtain confirmation or denial of the position (5.26, 5.27).

9.38 Economic substance should prevail over legal form (particularly in relation to off-balance sheet financing), but the legal position and its possible effects should be noted (5.28).

9.39 Window dressing should be outlawed and misleading accounts adjusted (5.29).

9.40 Accounting policies and Accounting Standards adopted should be explained in clear terms (5.34).

9.41 Financial statements should make clear what is distributable (5.40).

9.42 Information on the economic environment (referred to in paragraph 9.9(d) above) should include facts about the market and comparative operational statistics (5.41 – 5.44).

9.43 In line with paragraph 9.9(e) above, improved information should be given on directors and senior managers (5.45).

9.44 Information should be given in corporate reports on:
(a) responsibility for the financial statements;
(b) duties of audit committees; and
(c) responsibilities of the auditors (5.46).

9.45 A short discussion of managements' plans for staff requirements should be provided (5.48).

9.46 Conceptual problems with present financial statements could be overcome by:
(a) regular revaluations of fixed assets;
(b) writing down assets purely on the basis of loss of value;
(c) recognising unrealised gains in increases in financial wealth;
(d) re-establishing the primacy of the true and fair view;
(e) revealing all the components of changes in wealth in a single statement; and
(f) disclosing future plans and potential liabilities or gains (5.58).

LONG-TERM IMPROVEMENTS IN REPORTING INTERNALLY AND EXTERNALLY

9.47 As a result of our conclusion that "patching up" the present reporting regime would not be the ideal solution to existing deficiencies (1.17 and 5.2), we devised an entirely new package which we believed would be helpful to managements and, in somewhat abbreviated form, to external users. This package

Summary of Our Suggestions

forms the subject of Chapter 7, and we summarise our suggestions below.

9.48 The basic statements which we envisaged in the new package are:
  (a) an Assets and Liabilities Statement (7.12 – 7.20);
  (b) an Operations Statement (7.21 – 7.22);
  (c) a Statement of Changes in Financial Wealth (7.23 – 7.26); and
  (d) a Distributions Statement (7.27 – 7.32).

9.49 We suggested that changes in market capitalisation (suggested in paragraph 9.32 above) from period to period should be the subject of comment (7.15).

9.50 We thought it would be sensible for investors to be guided on the nature of the market capitalisation figure and to be given an indication of share price trends (7.16 – 7.17).

9.51 We believed that distributions should be permissible out of the increase in the financial wealth of an entity over the capital subscribed (adjusted for changes in the value of money) and subject to the cash resources and obligations of the entity (7.27 – 7.32).

9.52 We regarded Cash Flow Statements, both current and forward, as essential for directors; they should also be provided in modified form to external users (7.35 – 7.38 and 7.52).

9.53 We had further suggestions in relation to segmental reporting within the new package (7.39 – 7.42).

9.54 In Chapter 7, paragraph 7.53, we summarised the future-orientated documents which we believed to be necessary for managements and external users. These documents were discussed in more detail in paragraphs 7.7 to 7.10 inclusive and 7.46 to 7.52 inclusive. They are:
  (a) the Statement of Objectives (see paragraph 9.15 above) supported for managements only by a strategic plan;
  (b) a Financial Plan; and
  (c) Future Cash Flow Statements.

9.55 We suggested the "layering" method of presenting information for both internal and external purposes (7.54).

VALUATION OF ASSETS AND LIABILITIES

9.56 We referred in paragraph 9.2 above to our belief that value is a better basis than cost for displaying the worth of an entity, and in paragraph 9.4 to our preference for market (net realisable) values. We repeated these beliefs in Chapter 5 and suggested that it would facilitate the introduction of the package outlined in Chapter 7 if NRV were to be used for the periodical revaluation which we thought desirable in the shorter term for land and buildings (5.6, 5.7).

9.57 We used Chapter 6 for a discussion of the various methods of attributing figures to assets and liabilities. In particular we mentioned that, when using NRV, some assets might possess a nil value by themselves but the business units of which they formed a part did have a value. In such cases, both values should be disclosed (6.9 – 6.10).

9.58 Using NRV, we suggested that:
(a) valuation should be on the basis of orderly disposals;
(b) both assets and liabilities should be on that basis;
(c) allowance should be made for disposal costs; and
(d) individual assets and liabilities should be valued as far as practicable (6.27).

9.59 We also put forward practical considerations when applying values at NRV:
(a) for land, buildings and other fixed assets (6.28 – 6.29);
(b) for stocks and work-in-progress (6.31 – 6.32);
(c) for receivables, cash and bank balances (6.33);
(d) for investments (6.34); and
(e) for liabilities (6.35).

INDEPENDENT ASSESSMENT

9.60 Throughout the study we had at the back of our minds the need for an independent assessment of the information presented to external users of corporate reports. We explained our reasons for believing there to be a need (3.21) and our idea of the role which the independent assessor could play (3.22). We did not expect his role to extend to forming an opinion on the efficiency of management (3.23).

9.61 As regards more detailed matters, we thought that independent assessors ought to:
(a) judge the accuracy of managements' understandings about the influence of one company over another (5.26);
(b) form a view on the truth and fairness when off-balance sheet financing and window dressing occur (5.30);
(c) have their responsibilities explained in corporate reports (5.46 and 5.52);

Summary of Our Suggestions

    (d) report in long form, in plain, understandable terms, explaining how audits are conducted, their limitations, the responsibility of management for financial statements and for internal control, and that the opinion gives a reasonable assurance, not a guarantee (5.51 – 5.52);
    (e) highlight significant features of an entity's accounts in their reports and clearly spell out the problems when they have to qualify (5.53);
    (f) have their reports preceding the financial statements (5.53);
    (g) ensure that, as far as segmentalisation is concerned, investors are given a sensible split of the information provided (7.40);
    (h) consider in retrospect quarterly reports and "events" reporting (7.57); and
    (i) assess whether information included in the financial statements is comprehensible (7.65).

9.62 We suggested that audit committees, preferably drawn from non-executive directors, should be encouraged for all companies (5.56).

9.63 We did not foresee any technical difficulties for independent assessors in our new package outlined in Chapter 7, but we thought there would be a need for:
    (a) external assistance with some valuations;
    (b) multi-disciplinary audit teams;
    (c) continuous monitoring of computerised information;
    (d) reporting to an external regulator if there is a critical breakdown in an information system; and
    (e) a long-form *ad hoc* report from the independent assessor (7.59 – 7.67) – and see also paragraph 9.61(d) above.

RESEARCH NEEDED

9.64 In the course of our study we identified certain specific areas which we thought would benefit from research and experimentation. These are:
    (a) management performance reviews (3.23);
    (b) the use of present values of future cash flows to assess the real worth of entities (5.20 – also discussed in 6.7);
    (c) managements' responsibilities for disclosing the consequences of significant fraud, illegality or incompetence (5.35);
    (d) the means and usefulness of reporting the materiality basis used by managements and auditors (5.36);

Making Corporate Reports Valuable

(e) reporting the worth of personnel to an entity (5.50 – following discussion in 5.47 – 5.49);

(f) the nature and possibility of assigning values to the "assets" which make up the difference between the net identifiable assets and the market capitalisation of an entity (7.13);

(g) the implications for discipline, training and quality control of multi-discipline assessment teams (7.61); and

(h) the benefits and costs of our proposals (8.20; 8.26).

9.65 The foregoing are just the individual areas that occurred to us as worthy of research projects. As we explained in the Introduction, we hope that the whole document will stimulate discussion and experimentation (0.2) and particularly our suggested package in Chapter 7 and our views on valuation in Chapter 6 (0.10).

APPENDIX

Vocabulary and Abbreviations

To help avoid misunderstandings, the following are the meanings which we attach, for the purposes of this discussion document only, to some of the terms we use. They are simple explanations in ordinary, everyday language and are not intended as legal or technical definitions.

Additivity – the total figure of numbers in a statement should not mean something different in kind from the individual numbers

Asset – something that an entity or an individual owns and that has a worth which is capable of being converted into cash

Corporate report – the whole package of information which boards of directors (or equivalents) provide to investors – usually annually

Economic reality – what in fact happens expressed, as far as practicable, in financial terms

Efficiency (of the market) – a state in which all traders have the same quality and quantity of information available to them

Entity – any business enterprise required by law to report periodically to its investors

Financial wealth – the quantifiable assets less the quantifiable liabilities of an entity or individual at a point in time (quantifiable, that is, in financial terms)

Investor – one who has invested or intends to invest. It can include existing or potential shareholders in, proprietors of, and long-term lenders to, an entity

Liability – something that an entity or individual owes and will at some time have to pay by surrendering an asset (usually cash)

Management – the directors (or equivalent) and senior managers of an entity, ie the top decision-taking level

Wealth – everything that an entity or individual owns or benefits from at a point in time, less everything that he, she or it owes at the same point

ABBREVIATIONS

Abbreviations have been kept to a minimum in this book, but we have found it helpful to use the following:

CCA	current cost accounting
CPP	current purchasing power
FASB	Financial Accounting Standards Board (USA)
HC	historical cost
ICI	Imperial Chemical Industries plc
NRV	net realisable value
P&L a/c	profit and loss account
RC	replacement cost
SSAP	Statement of Standard Accounting Practice